vaastu

THIS IS A CARLTON BOOK

Text and Design © Carlton Books Limited, 2001

This edition published by Carlton Books Limited, 2001

20 Mortimer Street

London, W1N 7RD

A CIP catalogue for this book is available from the British Library.

ISBN 1 84222 206 6

Executive Editor: Sarah Larter
Senior Art Editor: Diane Spender
Picture Researcher: Claire Gouldstone
Design and Editorial: Andy Jones, Barry Sutcliffe and Deborah Martin
Production: Janette Davis
Cover Designer: Alison Tutton

vaastu

the indian spiritual alternative to feng shui

Richard Craze

contents

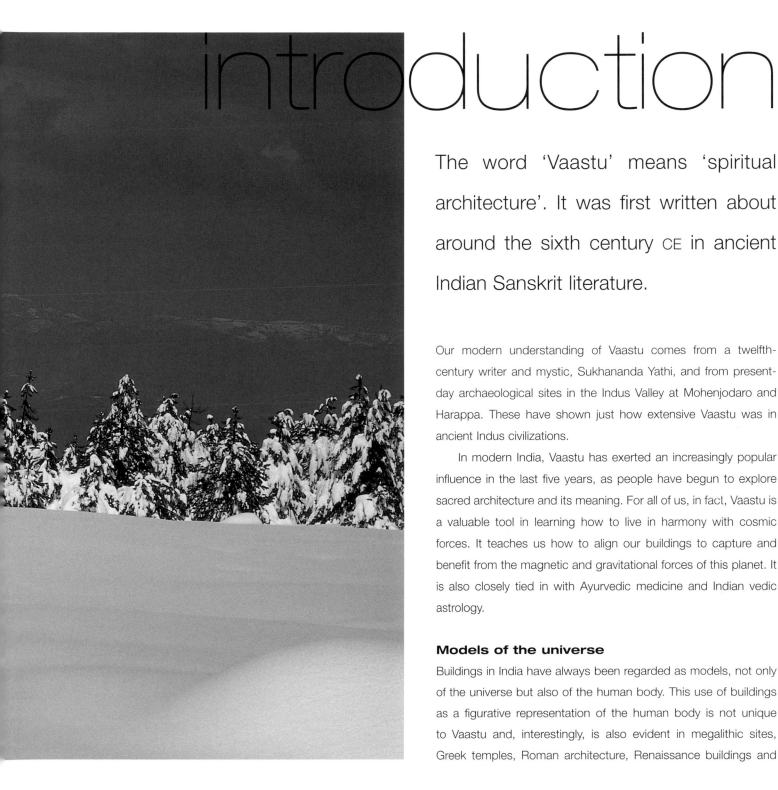

introduction

The word 'Vaastu' means 'spiritual architecture'. It was first written about around the sixth century CE in ancient Indian Sanskrit literature.

Our modern understanding of Vaastu comes from a twelfth-century writer and mystic, Sukhananda Yathi, and from present-day archaeological sites in the Indus Valley at Mohenjodaro and Harappa. These have shown just how extensive Vaastu was in ancient Indus civilizations.

In modern India, Vaastu has exerted an increasingly popular influence in the last five years, as people have begun to explore sacred architecture and its meaning. For all of us, in fact, Vaastu is a valuable tool in learning how to live in harmony with cosmic forces. It teaches us how to align our buildings to capture and benefit from the magnetic and gravitational forces of this planet. It is also closely tied in with Ayurvedic medicine and Indian vedic astrology.

Models of the universe

Buildings in India have always been regarded as models, not only of the universe but also of the human body. This use of buildings as a figurative representation of the human body is not unique to Vaastu and, interestingly, is also evident in megalithic sites, Greek temples, Roman architecture, Renaissance buildings and

especially in many Christian churches, which are built to represent the body of Christ on the cross.

In classic Vaastu architecture, as in Hindu, the ground plan of a temple – known as the *vaastupurusha mandala* – is laid out in a sacred, regular shape of 64 squares, in which the head, body and legs of a cosmic human are outlined. This symbolic universal figure is known as *purusha* – the seed or link. In Buddhist temples the holy relic of the Buddha himself would be located in the very centre – the heart of the *purusha*.

Vaastu and *feng shui*

As the popularity of architectural sciences such as *feng shui* grows, there is an increasing desire to discover how other cultures and other civilizations regard buildings and how they affect the environment. Here in the West *feng shui* (about which more later) has become very popular. There are currently over 320 books on

the subject in English alone and a quick search on the internet will give you over a thousand *feng shui* consultants offering a variety of services to improve your health, love life, sex life, wealth, luck, prosperity, even coping with your children. There is no doubt indeed that it is an extremely popular subject.

Vaastu is a kind of Indian equivalent. But the two are very different. If you have no experience at all of *feng shui* then don't worry because Vaastu stands alone and requires no previous experience of any architectural science.

So what is Vaastu?

Vaastu is a very ancient set of guidelines laid down to improve the way we live. It covers just about every aspect of house design and construction, including decor and decoration, furnishings and fabrics, siting of rooms, structure of the building, location of the building, direction the house should face, and size and dimensions

of the building. In fact there is no aspect of where and how we live that isn't covered. These guidelines obviously appertain to India and we shall have to modify them to suit a Western audience. For instance, a great deal is made in Vaastu of where you site your granary. Now, I don't know about you, but I personally have never felt the need for a granary. In Vaastu the granary should always be sited in the south-west. This area is warmer and dryer and stops fungal rot and damp getting into the corn. That's fine if you live in as hot a climate as India. But in the UK and most of the US these climatic principles simply don't apply. So we don't need a granary (unless you really want one, of course) and the weather is not quite so extreme and thus not quite so important.

Strictly speaking, Vaastu is an architectural science – it applies to how and where you build your house. The principles of Vaastu are taken into consideration before the first spade of earth is dug or the first brick laid. Now obviously we can't all commission our own house-building project simply on the strength of what someone was writing about several thousand years ago in India, so we have to adapt the principles to take that into consideration. Generally we already have our house and want to find out how to improve it rather than tear it down and start again.

Setting our objectives

Before we begin to learn about Vaastu we have to set our objective. What is it we want from this ancient Indian subject? Are we interested purely from a historical point of view? Or do we seek serious and practical help in improving our living arrangements? I believe that most people want practical stuff – the 'how-do-I-do-it-for-myself?' sort of advice. I have given many lectures and talks on *feng shui* and have never found

anyone really interested in the theory or the history. What people want is to know how to fix things, how to improve the way they live and how to incorporate it into their decor schemes without seeming too wacky or new age. And that is the tone I shall adopt for this book – a simple, practical guide to doing it for yourself.

Who am I to be writing this?

I am not Indian, nor have I lived in India. I don't profess to know everything about Vaastu – nor would I want to. I am a writer who believes that all information, all knowledge should be available to anyone who wants it. There are no secrets. And there is no mumbo-jumbo. If a subject can be covered logically and simply then I will do it. I try to avoid the superstitious, the fraudulent, the semi-religious and the plain, outright ridiculous. Previously I have written books on *feng shui*, which is a subject I have seen grow in popularity in the West until, sadly, it has now become divorced from its original roots.

A second chance

Let's start again with Vaastu. It is a sensible subject that offers sound and practical advice to anyone who wants to improve their home. That's it. It is that simple. It is about working with what we've got and making things better in terms of light, space, clarity and harmony. It isn't about superstition, nor is it based on religious belief. If it were, I wouldn't have been interested in researching it so deeply over the past few years.

What does Vaastu involve?

Vaastu is very different from *feng shui* in that it makes us look as closely at ourselves as at the fabric or construction of our home. In *feng shui*, if you are able to get the energy moving right it is assumed that this will affect you beneficially. In Vaastu more emphasis is placed on working on the person at the same time, rather than just hoping or assuming that they will improve. Vaastu is a much more integrated and holistic subject.

The principles of Vaastu apply as much to the occupants of a house as they do to the bricks and mortar. Before you embark on a course of Vaastu you should examine your own motives, lifestyle, health and aspirations. You can't expect Vaastu to put right everything in your life if you aren't prepared to make considerable effort yourself to improve your situation. Vaastu doesn't work independently. It works hand in hand with the individual to help each one take positive steps towards improving their life. Vaastu is a set of guidelines that apply to both the home and the person. It works with three principle tools:

- *Shastra* (house design, location and siting)
- *Ayurveda* (your health and lifestyle, including diet and fitness)
- *Jyotish* (the astrological information appertaining to when you were born)

These three key ingredients make up the recipe that brings about change. Simply by looking at ourselves we will find that a lot of what is wrong becomes self-evident. By examining how we live we can make changes to improve our lives. Here we will look very

briefly at these three ingredients; they will be examined in greater detail later in the book.

Shastra

Shastra means skill or art form. The skill in putting together a house, a building or architectural structure of any sort is purely physical. Build it wrongly and it falls down. Build it from cheap, shoddy materials and the occupants will suffer. Build it in a bad place and it will flood or rot or collapse. Build it in the right way, out of the right materials and in the right place and the occupants will thrive and prosper. *Shastra* also deals with the way energy – *prana* (universal breath) – moves through buildings (and ourselves, of course) and the way the magnetic forces of the Earth affect us.

Ayurveda

If the occupants eat badly, take no exercise and ignore health warnings they will get sick. *Ayurveda* is a set of guidelines for healthy living. It makes sense to look after ourselves and to be healthy. *Ayurveda* is a simple means whereby we can prevent disease and remain healthy by following these simple guidelines.

Jyotish

This deals with astrology. When you were born influences what sort of person you are and the way in which living in a particular house can affect you. This is an enormously important part of Indian culture. We in the West might dismiss this as superstitious nonsense for the gullible but there is no doubt that the planets exert considerable influence over us – you only have to look at what the Moon does to the tides.

Technically the astrological part of Vaastu isn't true astrology in the sense that you don't need a detailed chart drawn up and it contains no specific predictions or character analysis. All *jyotish* is concerned with is your rising sign – what planet was appearing over the horizon at the moment of your birth. This indicates what planet exerts the most influence on you and can affect your mental outlook and direction in life. In the West we know we are Leo or Cancer or whatever as this is the constellation that the Sun was passing through at the time of our birth. But in India it is considered of secondary importance. What is significant is your rising sign. We will, of course, look at this in much more detail later.

Why Vaastu and not Vastu?

You will sometimes see Vaastu spelt with only one 'a'. But they are two different words and not to be confused. *Vaastu* means physical and material buildings. *Vastu*, on the other hand, means space or energy – that which fills up the building and is invisible and subtle. The two go hand in hand because as soon as you have constructed a room out of bricks and mortar – the *vaastu* – you have at once also created the *vastu* of the room – the space and energy. But they remain different.

The Vaastu consultant

Vaastu consultants are beginning to appear. Traditionally they were known as *shilpi* and were brought in at the design stage of a building. They were a sort of spiritual architect and important because they could prevent buildings being built on unsuitable

recurring worries or major life problems, then it might just be that your environment is making you sick. Of course the cause might lie elsewhere, such as at work, but it could be that the influences of your home are holding you back. If you are buoyant, happy and positively charged then the chances are that Vaastu will do little to enhance an already good outlook. If you feel you need help Vaastu is a useful tool. It isn't the only one, though, and mustn't become an obsession. Vaastu puts you back on the road but it isn't the road itself. It is a kind of signpost to recovery but you have to do a lot of work yourself. In Vaastu there are no quick fixes, no simple remedies, no instant cures. Only by diligently and carefully examining all aspects of your lifestyle can you find out what is wrong.

sites. Once the building was finished, so was their job. They didn't forecast or correct defects. They were involved in the design and construction stages only. Once an occupant had moved in they had nothing further to do with the building. Nowadays, however, the *shilpi* seem to be diagnosing all sorts of building ailments and diseases that affect the occupants of a house – some of which hadn't even been discovered when Vaastu was first written about.

If you call in a *shilpi* (or Vaastu consultant, as they like to be called) make sure they aren't jumping on a bandwagon. To be blunt, some of them can be horribly pessimistic when it comes to your house and what it is doing to you. They can predict all sorts of ill health and fatal accidents happening. And all you have to do is hand over lots of money and they can put it all right for you. I leave it to you to decide whether they are genuine or charlatans.

How do I know if I need Vaastu?

If you suffer constant ill health, apathy, lack of appetite, depression, sleeplessness, irritability, gloominess, lack of energy,

How this book works

What we shall do here is look at the three key stages of Vaastu, starting with the *shastra*, then the *ayurveda* and finally the *jyotish*. Each has a lot of information in it which may initially seem unrelated. Only later will we tie the three strands together in order to make the whole subject become clear. Vaastu takes all three key elements of mind, body and soul and fuses them into a new and exciting way of arranging our environment and ourselves to maximize our potential. In a sense you have already taken the first major step. By seeking change, you will find that change occurs. Do nothing and stagnation is inevitable. Now you have taken the first step, the rest should be easy.

a history of Vaastu
and the
sacred
architecture
of other
cultures

The sacred architecture of Vaastu has links with other sacred architecture from other cultures.

What may at first glance seem to be arbitrary principles become clearer when we see that many other cultures and civilizations have independently arrived at very similar conclusions. It is as if humans have certain fundamental needs regarding how and where they live. If these needs are met they feel happy and flourish. If these needs are not met they tend to decline.

Angkor Wat, Cambodia, is a fine example of a tomb for dead kings and a building constructed for quiet contemplation of a spiritual existence.

The *vaastushastra*

The word 'Vaastu' comes from the Sanskrit word *vaas,* which means 'habitat'. Vaastu is the science of constructing a habitat. As a science it is traceable to sixth-century Indian Sanskrit literature but has largely lain dormant until recent years. Up until some ten years ago the only comprehensive literature available was an ancient Sanskrit text – *vaastushastra* – by Sukhananda Yathi, written during the twelfth century CE.

There is however quite a considerable body of evidence from historical and archaeological sources. Recent excavations at Mohenjodaro and Harappa in India have revealed considerable Vaastu influences on the Indus Valley civilizations.

According to the ancient texts, the selection of a site is the most important aspect of Vaastu. The ideal site is always square-shaped. This is the most recurring theme in Vaastu and one we shall return to later in the practical sections, but it is worth keeping in mind. *Feng shui* works more with circular shapes, curves and gentle slopes. Vaastu is primarily concerned with squares, straight lines and right angles.

The earth grid

So, the ideal site is a square with open space all around it. Ideally it should slope towards the north-east and the ground level should be highest at the south-west corner. The reason for this seems to be that energy lines have been found to run across the surface of the planet forming a grid around the earth. This energy is aligned along a north/south axis and again east/west. To ensure maximum benefit from these energy paths one should align one's home with them – placing a square along this grid of energy.

Any irregular shapes seem to upset the flow of energy. Likewise regular, but not square shapes, such as triangles, rectangles and octagons, also seem to decrease the benefit to be had from the energy. This energy would appear to be magnetic and there is considerable evidence that the sites of Shiva temples were always selected for their very high magnetic fields. These high magnetic fields have considerable healing properties.

Like this temple in India, most spiritual buildings soar upwards to lead our eyes and thoughts to heaven.

Ancient texts

Nowadays we talk about magnetic fields but in ancient texts the word used is always *prana* – universal breath. We will look at exactly how this is interpreted later. The ancient texts are scriptures of which there are two types – *Sruti* and *Smrti*. *Sruti* consists of the four *Vedas* – holy works (from the Sanskrit *ved* – to know) – which are taken to be the word of Brahma himself through the Lord Krishna. The *sruti* is never written down, it is sung as a song which is remembered by sages. *Smrti* on the other hand is written down in Sanskrit and can be added to or adapted as times and traditions change. The *smrti* is a series of books giving religious and social guidance on a variety of subjects, including Vaastu and *ayurveda*, but they take their inspiration from the *sruti*.

Vaastu elsewhere

It is sometimes difficult to determine where Vaastu ends and *feng shui* begins – or the other way round – as the lines are becoming blurred. Indian Vaastu consultants are borrowing heavily from *feng shui* to make their adaptations more palatable to a Western audience. But recently an unusual link was made between sacred Indian architecture and ancient buildings in Latin America. In 1995 Ganapati Sthapati, one of India's leading traditional temple architects, confirmed that the layout of two ancient Incan structures at Machu Picchu high in the Andes mountains conform completely to the principles of Vaastu. These two buildings, a temple and a house, use the very same layouts, location for doors and windows, proportions of width to length, roof styles and degrees of roof slopes, column sizes and wall thicknesses. The residential layout is very similar to that of a building excavated at Mohenjodaro in India. The temple layout resembles temples being built in India to this day.

You may wonder how this can be. Well, in the original text on Vaastu *shastra* which is dated around 8000 BCE the authorship is attributed to one Mayamatam and the name – as

The eagle stands guard over steps leading to the sacred temple of the Toltecs.

Mayan – crops up repeatedly throughout all the ancient texts. So Mayan was writing about Vaastu many thousand of years ago and in ancient Mayan architecture we find remarkable similarities. The name Mayan also crops up in ancient Tamil scriptures and he is even claimed to be the author of *Surya Siddhanta* which is one of the most ancient Hindu texts on astronomy. Mayan advocated the use of the modular form of building, whereby you take an eight by eight square to give a unit of 64 to work with – a bit like a chess board. This floor grid is important to Vaastu, as we will see later. This 64-square module is known as the *vaastupurusha mandala*. On close inspection the Incan and Mayan architecture used this module as well.

And it isn't just the size and shape of the buildings that have so many similarities. Even the sculptures are closely related. In Mayan decorative work there is a very common feature – the mask, as it is known to modern archaeologists – but to the lay person it is the Big Nose. In India temple sculptures also have this feature – a deity placed at the top of an arch with a nearly identical face, known in the Hindi language as *Maha Nyasa*, which translates as Big Nose.

In Mayan architecture many sculptures contain other features which are almost identical, including earrings, buckles, teeth, head-dresses and even priests sitting meditating in the lotus position.

So what's the connection? Well, we don't know for sure. Could Mayan have been an early Indian architect who liked to travel? India had double-hulled catamarans capable of long sea voyages prior to this time, similar to the one the Norwegian Thor Heyerdahl used to make his journey from Africa to Peru in the 1970s. And remember that Sanskrit was the only language that didn't have to find a word for the modern invention of the aeroplane. It already had a word for 'aircraft' that dates back to 8000 BCE.

Pointing skywards

But it isn't just the Mayans and the Indians that use sacred architecture. Virtually every civilization has had some form of divine ritualized building that had to be laid out to certain prescribed principles. From the very earliest times people have believed that the universe contains much more than the world immediately surrounding us. They have pointed skywards and wondered what gods reside there. Temples are built to represent some form of earthly heaven, a desire to replicate the order of the cosmos, an attempt to recreate paradise on Earth. In many cultures, particularly within India and China, heaven is represented by the circle and earth by the square.

Quartering the circle

Many ancient civilizations believed that sacred architecture captured the essence of the deity within it as long as it followed the principles they had evolved. Romulus founded the city of Rome by cutting into the ground a circle around the Palatine Hill. He called this circle *mundus* – the world – and he divided it into four quarters, just as we quarter the globe into north, south, east and west. After that every new Roman city was started by a priest drawing a circle in the earth and quartering it. The lines always ran from east to west and north to south. The line from east to west represented the course of the sun and the north/south line was the axis of the sky. This primitive grid was projected out into the future city to plan roads and networks.

From dark to light

Many sacred buildings, from megalithic graves to Jewish synagogues, face the rising sun as a source of new life and power.

Myanmor temple. Virtually all civilizations build sacred architecture based on the square and rising to the sky.

Most Christian churches are aligned in a similar fashion. You enter from the west and walk to the altar at the east – moving from dark to light, from death to new life.

Entire Chinese cities were laid out along the same four-line grid but they used south as their 'best' direction. Native American Indian sweat lodges are always aligned with their entrance facing east so the first rays of the new sun can enter the lodge as Tirawa – the morning star.

Reaching for the stars

Once you have aligned your sacred building you can build upwards. A lot of early cultures use the square as a base – the symbol of Earth – and then build upwards into a circular style to attain heaven on top of the Earth. Examples can be seen in the Buddhist temples at Borobudur in central Java, Angkor in Cambodia and Pagan in Burma. They all follow the classic principle of the square base surmounted by terraces, followed by circular levels. Travellers climb the temple, ascending from material Earth to spiritual heaven as they do so. Gothic spires are designed to lead the eye upwards to heaven in the sky. Many primitive people regarded mountains as sacred since they allowed one to climb higher to the gods. Caves were representative of the darkness of earthly existence.

Pagodas and Zen temples all have the same purpose – to raise our consciousness to the heavens and cosmos above. Temples are places where the divine may be encountered. In the Christian religion the term for a church is literally 'house of god'. It is not that God resides there but that God may be found there by those who seek such an encounter. In Hindu temples Krishna is represented in human form and the temple is literally again the home of God.

ABOVE: The spires of Chartres Cathedral were amongst the first great Gothic expressions of spirituality.

LEFT: The totem pole, thrusting upwards, is a link between earth and sky.

Choosing a temple site

To choose a site for a temple different cultures have different procedures, but they all inevitably rely on a set of guidelines laid down by the priesthood. In China the Taoist priest will use *feng shui* (*feng* – wind, *shui* – water) to determine the most auspicious location for a temple. The priest always looks for a site where the energy – *chi* – flows positively. *Chi* is capable of being carried away and dispersed if the site is too windy, or to stagnate if the site is too still. *Feng shui* relies heavily on the *pah kwa* compass – this designates auspicious sites according to the direction in which they face. The compass school of *feng shui* is based on the principles of the five elements (wood, earth, fire, metal, water). Each of these five elements is associated with a compass direction and also linked to shapes, landscape characteristics, buildings and colours. South is fire, west is metal, east is wood, north is water and the centre is earth.

The history of *feng shui*

Feng shui has been around in China for at least as long as people have lived in houses. There are several very ancient books that outline its fundamental principles and explain its workings, ranging from the *Shih Ching* (Book of Songs) compiled between the ninth and fifth centuries BCE to the *Li Chi* (Record of Rites) developed during the Han dynasty (206 BCE–220 CE).

More modern works have included the *Ku Chin T'u Shu Chi Ch'eng* (Imperial Encyclopaedia), a 1726 edition of which is in the British Museum. However, the first reports of *feng shui* to arrive in the West were towards the end of the nineteenth century when missionaries first visited China on a regular basis. They were somewhat surprised that there was already an ancient and well-developed religion in place, Taoism, which was closely bound up with *feng shui*. And they were taken aback when they were not allowed to erect any Christian crosses. It was bad *feng shui*, they were told, to stab the land.

In mainland China, *feng shui* was practised extensively until Chairman Mao's Cultural Revolution, which started in 1949 and lasted for nearly twenty years. During that time all ancient cultural practices were violently discouraged by the regime. Since the easing of government authority *feng shui* is making a rapid return.

Modern *feng shui*

In Hong Kong, Singapore, Taiwan and other places not subject to the oppression of the Cultural Revolution, *feng shui* has been practised continuously. Today it has a valid place in modern building design and *feng shui* principles have been observed in the design of some important new sites, including the Bank of China building in Hong Kong and the Hong Kong and Shanghai Bank.

The Bank of China. This is a good example of the old philosophy of feng shui *working in harmony with modern architecture.*

The Hyatt Hotel in Singapore has reported a considerable upturn in business since it adapted its building to improve the *feng shui*.

Many businesses operating in both the East and the West are seeing the value of the principles of *feng shui* being incorporated into building design and decor. They include Citibank, Morgan Bank, Chase Manhattan Bank and the Asian *Wall Street Journal* offices.

As in Vaastu, the ideal building in *feng shui* is a square shape. Although the Chinese regard the circle as more sacred, they have conceded that square buildings are much easier to design and build – and easier to live in, of course.

Egyptian sacred architecture

For most of us the pyramids are an ideal representation of what the ancient Egyptians would regard as sacred architecture. They have the obligatory square base and rise to a sharp point to lead us heavenwards again. They too are constructed using a grid

system; each Egyptian measurement is supposed to represent one of the three sacred numbers – 3, 4, 5.

- 3 is the number of heaven.
- 4 is the number of Earth.
- 5 the number of humankind.

The square base with its four sides is the symbol for Earth and materialism. The base is said to be divided into twelve smaller squares to represent the twelve astrological signs and the twelve parts of the human body – head, chest, belly, genitals, two arms, two legs, two hands and two feet. This is also a theme used in Vaastu, and one which we shall look at presently.

The Christian church and the body of Christ

In Christian churches there is a similar representation of the human body. The body of Christ is said to represent everyman and the

We cannot even begin to contemplate the labour needed to build the pyramids – only wonder at the driving force that led to their creation.

church is designed as his body on the cross. Mass is celebrated at the head, with the aisles as the arms and the nave as the body on the cross. The Byzantine churches use a more abstract symbolism, with the nave being the body, the chancel the soul and the altar the spirit.

In Vaastu a similar symbolism is used: a square ground plan is divided into 64 smaller squares, with a human form invisibly overlaid on it to represent the cosmic human (see page 51).

Islam and mosques

Mosques are laid out in a similar fashion, with a square base surmounted by an ornate dome. According to Islam, Allah is everywhere so the mosque doesn't so much contain God, as, say, a Christian church, but is instead a meeting place for believers and God or a prayer room where people might call upon God. The whole source of religious inspiration in a mosque is its space. Internally there are no walls, or at least only a minimum of internal supports. The devotee is encouraged to contemplate the open space.

Buddhism and stupas

The principal sacred architecture of Buddhism is the stupa – a large domed structure said to contain a fragment of the Buddha himself. Buddhists have taken the symbolism of the human form even further and incorporated some relic of a real human within the structure. These relics may be claimed to be from the Buddha or from a holy saint or monk. Stupas first began to be built in some numbers around the third century BCE and were covered in carvings representing significant events in the life of the Buddha. Invariably a stupa will have thirteen tiers to its steeple to represent

the thirteen Buddhist heavens. The stupa is built, again, on a square base.

The Roman pantheon

But it isn't just in the East where sacred architecture has been used. The Pantheon in Rome was built by the Emperor Hadrian around 120 CE. It is a conventional temple with a porch leading to a massive circular hall surmounted by a half-sphere of perfect dimensions – if it was a complete sphere it would exactly touch the ground as a giant ball. In the centre of the sphere is a hole to allow rain and snow to fall into the building and to land on the marble floor; the hole represents the all-seeing eye of the god. In 610 the Pantheon became the first pagan temple in Rome to be taken over by Christians. It is still a centre for Christian worship.

The megalithic builders

Additionally, sacred architecture is not confined to any one time. The megalithic builders, who were constructing their stone avenues and circles around the fifth to the second millennia BCE, were probably trying to express some aspect of sacred architecture. They built square-shaped burial chambers by using upright stones supporting horizontal slabs.

Megalithic monuments are not confined to Europe, although many of the best sites are certainly found there – at Stonehenge and Avebury in England, for instance, Carnac in France and New Grange in Ireland. Others are found as far afield as Bali, Polynesia, India, Mexico and Tahiti. They all perform a range of functions, including astronomical observatories, funeral sites, meeting

ABOVE: Domes surmount the Blue Mosque, Istambul.
RIGHT: Bodhgaya (Bihar, India), the site of the Buddha's enlightenment.

LEFT: The Pantheon.
RIGHT: Stonehenge.

places and centres for worship. But all of them are constructed to serve humankind in its constant endeavour to become more closely acquainted with the universal spirit of the cosmos.

A need for spiritual fulfilment

This need or desire for contact with the spirit world is a primordial and essential part of our make-up. We are material beings housing the essence of the spirit and we have a fundamental need to become reunited with our soul. Collectively this is done through sacred architecture. But individually there is still a driving need to pursue this within the boundaries of our own home. How and where we live needs to reflect this desire to be spirit beings. If we live entirely in the material world we stagnate and become grounded. If we encourage our soul to soar and reunite with the cosmos we expand and grow spiritually and creatively.

Vaastu sets out ground rules for doing this within our home. By focusing on how we live, we encourage our consciousness to expand to fill the space. By creating a tranquil and serene sanctuary, we derive more pleasure from our home and are better able to reach our true potential.

Tying it all together

Throughout this brief excursion into other cultures' sacred architecture several themes seem to recur: the square base; the principle of a special place dedicated to communing with our spirit selves; a lofty symbolism to encourage us to look upwards and into the heart of the cosmos. These are all themes we will look at in our study of Vaastu.

a brief history
of India

Before we can begin to look at the principles of Vaastu we need to have a brief look at the history of India itself.

The reason for this is that it will help our study if we understand how India has developed over the centuries. For instance, when I first began to study Vaastu I wondered how such an important architectural science could have anything to offer when India was obviously such a poor country in many ways. My thinking was that if Vaastu is so beneficial why hasn't it done much for the poor masses of India? There were two things I failed to realize at that time. The first was that Vaastu has lain dormant for a very long time and isn't in current or popular use even in its home country. And secondly, the poor of India are a relatively modern phenomenon, largely as a result of the country's colonization by various other cultures and civilizations, chief of which of course were the British.

Clearly, understanding something of the history enables us to see India in greater depth. Over the years various invasions have brought tremendous diversity and complexity to the culture of India. Yet many of the ancient and unique features have remained surprisingly recognizable throughout her history. However, as

Dance and music – as in this temple in India – are common forms of expression throughout the world and can help us celebrate a ritualized approach to spiritual growth and development.

different cultures have been absorbed into India's civilization, they have had an effect on the country's art, architecture, religious beliefs and politics. Today the most apparent evidence of such diversity has been the splitting up of the original extent of India into three parts – India, Bangladesh and Pakistan.

We must remember that India covers a large area and is also extremely diverse. Evidence indicates that there were at least two distinct cultures in ancient India and that they merged at different times and in different ways. To understand Vaastu fully, we have to examine how these different cultures borrowed from each other since facets of each bring something new and unique to Vaastu.

India is a country of intense extremes and incredible beauty.

The Indus civilizations

The Indus, or Harappa, civilization, one of the most advanced of ancient times, was similar in many ways to cultures in Mesopotamia. Harappa culture flourished until about 1500 BCE, when the Indus Valley was overrun by Aryan invaders from the Iranian plateau. The mainly nomadic Aryans spoke an archaic form of Sanskrit and left little behind in the way of remains or archaeological evidence that we can see today. But they did leave their scriptures – the *Vedas*. These, as we saw earlier, were not

intended to be written down but rather were recited or sung. They were passed from sage to sage as each learnt them in perfect order.

The *Vedas* also mention the division of society into *varnas*, or classes, from which evolved the caste system still current in India today. The *Vedas* and the caste system are part of the basis of Hinduism, which is both a religion and a social system. Despite the fact that they built no cities and contributed nothing to the art of India, the Aryans have left behind an important legacy in the way they have shaped India's thinking and habits.

The Aryans were an aggressive people who rode horses and expanded their territory ever southwards, pushing back much of north India's indigenous population of smaller darker people. The Aryans called these people *dasas* but they are known as Dravidians today.

No one can accurately date the arrival of the Dravidians in southern India, but we know that they were forced south by the Aryans. Modern India is still racially divided into two quite distinct types, and cultural differences between north and south India remain today. Aryan religious texts indicate that the Aryans viewed themselves as racially and culturally superior and reviled the *dasas*. In the north, the area of Aryan dominance, the name *dasa* eventually came to mean slave.

Over the centuries pre-Aryan and Aryan cultures gradually fused in northern India as the Aryans pushed slowly eastwards towards the plain of the River Ganges. This is where the second of ancient India's great urban civilizations developed. Such cities as

The bathers cast off their sin in the sacred River Ganges then climb the steps to a purer existence.

Pataliputra (near modern Patna), Kasi (modern Varanasi), and Ajodhya were founded by the Aryans who had by now become part of India itself and were no longer mere invaders. These cities grew immensely until they became the most important trading and religious centres in all of India. Today Varanasi is still a centre for pilgrimage by Hindus, who come to bathe in the River Ganges. Many of the pilgrims are sick or elderly and they come to Varanasi to die, for it is regarded as the most sacred of all places. For three miles the river is lined with steps to enable the countless thousands who come here to bathe. Behind the steps are shrines, towers and temples. Day and night funeral pyres burn so the ashes can be scattered into the river, enabling the souls of the faithful to be reborn in a favourable higher caste.

In the Bihar region in the sixth century BCE a wealthy merchant class, the *Vaishyas*, began to expand their influence and change the religious beliefs of the Aryans. The *Vedas* were added to in the form of the *Upanishads* – scriptural texts which sought to modify and update the original principles. In the north-east, where Aryan influence was relatively weak, the religions of Jainism and Buddhism were both founded.

In 326 BCE, Alexander the Great invaded the Indus Valley. India was still fragmented and there was no one capable of organizing sufficient forces to repel the invasion. However, the invasion faltered and was finally defeated by its own size, shortness of stores and the heat and disease of India. Shortly afterwards India's first large empire was founded by Chandra Gupta Maurya. His Maurya dynasty was based at Pataliputra. His grandson Asoka ruled an empire that extended to the south of central India's Deccan Plateau and west into Baluchistan and modern Afghanistan; in the east it included the state of Kalinga, which he had conquered in 261 BCE.

Asoka also attempted to create a state religion incorporating Buddhism and other faiths as well as Hinduism. A convert to Buddhism, he sent Buddhist missionaries abroad and is credited with elevating Buddhism to a world religion, although eventually it declined as a separate belief system within India.

Under the Mauryas and succeeding dynasties, for a period of about 800 years, India evolved a civilization that still remains fairly intact. The institution of caste was solidly implanted, and Hindu philosophy and legal codes were developed.

TOP: Young novice Buddhist monks.
ABOVE: Sitting under the Bodhi Tree – even in the harmony of nature we are drawn to spiritual architecture to complement and enhance.

The Gupta dynasty and the medieval period

The era of the Gupta dynasty which flourished from around 320 CE to 540 CE is generally considered to be ancient India's classical period. Indian architecture, sculpture, painting, dance and music thrived and expanded. Despite classical standards, however, many variations also came into being, primarily because of the numerous invasions of India by peoples from central Asia.

After the greatness of the Gupta dynasty, India entered its medieval period, becoming divided politically into a number of small kingdoms. This continued until the founding of the Mogul Empire in the sixteenth century.

Among the smaller states that appeared in India in the confusion of the seventh, eighth, and ninth centuries were the military aristocracies of the Rajputs in northern and central India. Racially, culturally and linguistically distinct Dravidian kingdoms also flourished in southern India, where these races settled after the Aryans forced them from the north. Most prominent were the kingdom of the Andhras, located in the areas around present-day Hyderabad; the Tamil states of the Pandyas at the southern tip of the Indian peninsula; the Cholas, in the region that is now Madras; and the Cheras, who controlled the south-western coast. From these local kingdoms many Indian ideas and practices spread to Indonesia and other parts of South-east Asia. The Pallava dynasty, which sponsored limited colonization throughout the area and played a dominant role in south-east India from the sixth to the eighth centuries, although of uncertain genealogy, was most likely Brahman and northern Indian in origin. Through the Pallavas, who were patrons of the arts, elements of Indo-Aryan Sanskrit culture were widely introduced into southern India.

Despite the fundamental unity of Indian civilization, political diversity was the rule during the medieval period. But cultural unity was still an underlying theme because of the shrines and pilgrimage sites throughout the subcontinent and the great body of Sanskrit oral tradition and myth. Cultural unity was also fostered by the co-operation between the Brahman religious leaders and political leaders.

Islam

Islam first entered the Indian subcontinent in 711 CE, when a young Arabian general, Muhammad ibn Qasim, invaded the Indus Valley. The state of Sind became part of Arabia and its people converted to Islam, but the Muslims did not advance deeper into India. In the ninth and tenth centuries, the contact with Arab traders in port cities along the south-west coast resulted in many Hindus converting to Islam. Cultural influences were transmitted in both directions. Baghdad scholars were especially intrigued by Indian mathematics, astrology and other sciences.

The chief Muslim conquerors of India were not Arabs, however, but central Asian converts to Islam – Turks, Afghans, Persians and Mongols – who began to enter the subcontinent around 1000 CE. The Muslims eventually converted many low-caste Hindus and Buddhists, particularly in Bengal and other eastern areas, as they moved across India.

The first Muslim Empire based in India was established in Delhi in 1206 by Qutb-ud-Din Aybak. This sultanate was part of a constantly expanding and contracting empire and was ruled by a line of 34 successive sultans. But that too came to an end in 1399 when Timur invaded from Samarkand during the Tughlug dynasty. He founded the Lodi kingdom, which lasted until 1526, and this new empire stretched from the Punjab in the west to the Bihar region in the east.

The Moguls

The first ruler of the Mogul dynasty was Babur, who claimed the subcontinent as his right of inheritance because of the conquest of Delhi by his ancestor Timur. Babur founded his new kingdom in 1526 but ruled for only four years. He was a highly intelligent and cultured Persian who didn't take to many aspects of Indian life but nonetheless established the most glorious empire in India's history.

Babur was deposed by his son, Humayun, who reigned from 1530 to 1540 and again in 1555–6 despite tremendous opposition from the Afghan Sher Shah, who ruled north India for five years.

In 1556 Humayin was succeeded by Akbar, whom history records as the greatest of all the Mogul emperors. He created the vast administrative organization that forms the basis for many present-day practices in India. A tolerant man, Akbar abolished a discriminatory tax on Hindus and did much to combine Hindu and Muslim motifs in palace architecture, art, literature and music.

Akbar's son and successor, Jahangir, introduced concepts of luxury and splendid living that had previously been unheard of in India. And his son, Shah Jahan, embarked on a massive and quite spectacular building programme that culminated in the Taj Mahal. Shah Jahan was also instrumental in extending the Mogul Empire to the Deccan plateau. After the death in 1707 of Aurangzeb, who can be considered the last of the great Mogul emperors, the Mogul Empire fell apart quickly, although ineffective rulers remained on the throne at Delhi until 1858.

The Europeans in India

Extensive European contact with India began in 1498 when Vasco da Gama, a Portuguese navigator, landed with three small ships at Calicut, on the south-west coast. Both the Portuguese and the Dutch attempted to colonize India during the sixteenth century, but neither

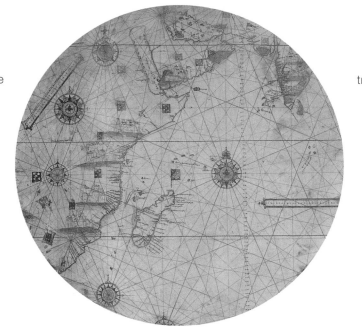

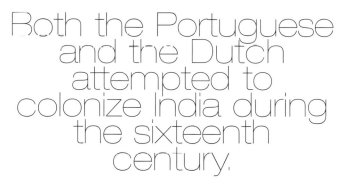

Both the Portuguese and the Dutch attempted to colonize India during the sixteenth century.

trading empire in India. The government-run French East India Company from 1664 onwards never really succeeded in generating a trade comparable to that of the British. In the eighteenth century both Britain and France sought to protect their trading interests by joining with native princes to fill the growing power vacuums created as the Mogul Empire disintegrated.

The two European powers came into conflict in India in 1746, when the French seized Madras. However, in 1761, during the Seven Years War, the French surrendered their territory of Pondicherry to the British, and after the peace treaty of 1763

proved strong enough to maintain the naval presence necessary to rival the British and French. The more tolerant Dutch concentrated on building a trading monopoly, through their Dutch East India Company.

The East India Company

The British Empire in India was established by a private trading firm, the East India Company (founded in 1600), which governed with the consent of Parliament until 1858. The company bought a strip of sandy beach at Madras in 1639, acquired a lease to the port of Bombay from King Charles II in 1668, and in 1690 secured from the Mogul emperor Aurangzeb permission to build a settlement on a muddy flatland that eventually became Calcutta.

The French got off to a slow start in their attempt to build a

the French retained only a few trading centres in India. The British were able to defeat the French largely because the British East India Company had a better navy, greater flexibility, and more reliable funding than the French East India Company.

The hero of Britain's battles against the French, Robert Clive, was a military adventurer who had started as a teenage clerk with the East India Company in the 1740s. Victory at Plassey led to effective political control over the vast riches of the Ganges Valley in 1765, when the nawab surrendered to Clive the right to collect land revenue for most of eastern India.

The Regulating Act

Some of the directors of the East India Company initially demurred at the prospect of governing the eastern region, Bengal, preferring to set up puppet princes to administer the area while they exploited its wealth for their own private gain. To counter the growing corruption within the company and to reform the governance of India, Parliament passed the Regulating Act of 1773. Warren Hastings, governor of Bengal in 1772–3, helped to lay the administrative foundations for British rule under the provisions of this act. As India's first governor-general (1773–85), Hastings consolidated many of Clive's territorial gains.

Lord Cornwallis, governor-general of India from 1786 to 1793, established the legal, administrative and land-revenue codes that made British rule possible. He separated the administrative and commercial functions of the company, organized a prestigious civil service, raised salaries so that irregular profits were unnecessary, and established disciplinary measures that made it possible to curb private trade by company employees.

Carrying offerings in procession is a familiar feature of Indian festivals and ceremonies.

Because of his belief that considerable corruption stemmed from contact with Indians, Cornwallis excluded people of Indian origin from higher posts of government. This policy led, during the nineteenth century, to a widening socio-economic gap between the British and their Indian subjects, with British settlements taking on the character of prosperous English towns in the midst of increasingly squalid Indian slums. Indian poverty was exacerbated by a rapid spurt in population growth that followed the establishment of peace and the adoption of public health measures throughout the subcontinent. British unwillingness to allow large-scale industrialization within India further intensified poverty. (The British preferred a subordinate economic role for their colonies within the British imperial system – a system that helped Britain to become an industrialized world power.)

Tension and unrest

Lord Wellesley, governor-general from 1798 to 1805, launched a policy of expansion, which culminated in the mid-nineteenth century, when the East India Company controlled more than three-fifths of India, with the remaining two-fifths being run by 562 local princes who were clearly subordinates of the British raj (government). Coupled with British policies of expansionism and exclusivity, British insensitivity to Indian traditions and religious practices helped to increase tensions. Among the Indian higher classes resentment of British rule grew, especially during the regime (1848–56) of Lord Dalhousie, who attempted to modernize and westernize India. In 1857 many traditional groups, largely in north India, revolted, led by mutineers in the army. This violent and brutal Indian mutiny, or Sepoy Rebellion, was put down by the British in 1858. As a direct result of the revolt, the crown took over most of the functions of the British East India Company. The revolt also intensified widespread feelings of distrust between the Indians and the British. Such feelings deepened as both Indian poverty and British wealth became magnified during the next century.

Indian nationalist sentiments found expression early in the nineteenth century in the writings of Rammohun Roy, a religious reformer, who hoped that a modern state of India would combine the best of both Hindu and Western cultures. The first organizations attempting to reform British rule were also formed early in the century. In 1885 they were welded together in the Indian National Congress by a retired British civil servant, Allan Hume (1829–1912), and a number of prominent Bengali leaders.

Early in the twentieth century the British made some attempts to meet the Congress's demands by widening Indian political participation. However, the extreme wing of the Congress increasingly demanded *swaraj* (complete independence). At about the same time (1906) Muslim leaders, dissatisfied with Hindu dominance of the Congress, formed their own nationalist organization, the Muslim League.

Independence

Although India's various nationalist groups united temporarily in 1916 in support of Britain's First World War effort, the increasingly dominant militants were disappointed by Britain's gradual approach to its professed goal of eventual self-rule for India. British prestige fell precipitously in 1919 with the passage of laws restricting political activity and with the massacre of Indian civilians by British troops at Amritsar. During the 1920s the Congress acquired a mass base, the support of prominent Indians, and increasing militancy under the leadership of Mahatma Gandhi, who introduced the highly successful techniques of passive resistance (*satyagraha*) and civil disobedience. During the 1920s, however, Muslims staged a large-scale withdrawal from the Congress. During the Second World War the Muslims, led by Muhammad Ali Jinnah and now demanding their own independent state (Pakistan), supported the British. The Congress, however, insisted that Britain leave India. When Indians refused to co-operate in repelling the Japanese attack on the subcontinent in 1942, Britain arrested many leaders and outlawed the Congress. A group of extreme anti-British Indian nationalists, led by Subhas Chandra Bose, even fought on the Japanese side in Burma and India.

At the end of the war Britain agreed to self-rule for India. However, in the 1946 elections the Muslim League won most of the Muslim vote, and Gandhi was unsuccessful in preventing the partition of the subcontinent into Muslim and Hindu states. In August 1947, India and Pakistan achieved independence. The task of governing India fell to its first prime minister, Jawaharlal Nehru. Jinnah became governor-general of the Muslim nation of Pakistan, which was then comprised of two separate territories, East and West Pakistan.

That is a very condensed version of the subcontinent's history, but it shows how one must never assume anything about India. A Western view might well be one of a poor country of Hindus and Buddhists. But the bigger picture shows us that it is much more complex than that. This short history may help to clarify some of our preconceptions about India and enhance our understanding of Vaastu.

shastra the principles of vaastu

From our brief look at India's history we can see that Vaastu was probably an import from the *Vedas* of the Aryans. It is therefore very ancient.

This means that certain architectural and cultural aspects of modern living hadn't even been thought of when the principles were formulated. And some that are mentioned are now redundant. We shall examine the principles first and then see which are workable today and how we can adapt those which aren't.

So, we'll start by looking at the basic principles, but bear in mind that they were laid down many centuries ago. And of course they were intended for people living in India. In the West circumstances are very different and whilst we respect and appreciate the principles, we have to be realistic and work with what we've got in the way of buildings here. Also these principles are set out as an architectural science – they are put into place before you build your house. In an ideal world we could choose exactly where and how we were going to build a new home. But the chances are we are already living somewhere and seek only to make changes rather than to uproot and start again from scratch.

Whether we live in a sophisticated city home or a rustic log cabin, we still need to be aware of our environment and the way it affects us. We can begin by understanding the principles of Vaastu.

Choosing a site

Before building your home you have to select a site. The larger the building plot you can use, the better. Imagine you select a square plot – which is the ideal shape – then it should be situated with each of its straight sides along an east/west, north/south axis. The construction should take place in the south-west part of your plot, leaving more space in the east as compared to the west. Likewise you should leave more space in the north than in the south. The diagram below shows this principle.

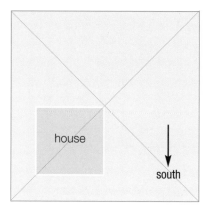

Siting the house in the south-west

If it is not possible to align the house in the south-west, then you should ensure that the east and north are at a lower level than the south and west. Also, the centre of the plot and the house should not be the same or overlap. Ideally the top left corner of the house (its north-east corner) should be directly central to the overall plot.

Water source

An ideal water source – a spring, well or borehole with an underground tank – would be located in the north-east part of the plot. If you have to use an overhead tank to store water it should be positioned somewhere along the western wall towards the south. See the diagram.

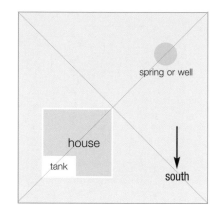

The position of the water source

Boundaries

The boundary wall along the south and west should be 1 foot (30 cm) higher than the north and east walls. For example, if the wall is 5 feet (150 cm) tall towards the north and east then it should be 6 feet (180 cm) tall in the south and west.

Entrance to the plot

The main entrance to the plot should not be directly in line with the front door of the house. These two should always be offset, otherwise whatever energy is in the house will simply flow straight out of the main gate.

Direction of your main gates

In the previous diagrams the house was located in its 'best' position in the south-west corner of the plot. This gives the owner large gardens to the north and east.

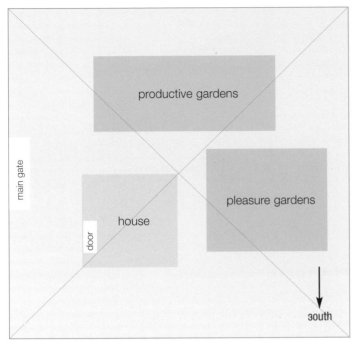

Position of main gates and gardens

Position your summerhouse to catch the best sunsets.

The two 'best' positions, then, for the main gate are along either the west wall or the south wall. Technically, to catch the evening sun, the west wall is considered better, but the south is fine. If the house is located in the south-west corner then north and east walls are considered not so good for the main gate. There are a lot of other permutations which we will look at later but let us for the moment assume than the new owner has decided on the west wall. The main gates should be positioned centrally along this wall. The main door of the house should then also be positioned on the west side of the house, as shown in the diagram above.

In an ideal world, the bulk of the gardens should be behind the house to ensure privacy and to catch the sunsets. The gardens should also catch the morning sun to bring new life and energy to the occupants. Gardens in the northern sector should be productive plots for fruit and vegetables, while in the east should be the pleasure gardens for relaxation and play.

Shape and direction of house

The square shape is good. It allows us to be grounded in reality and surrounds us with harmony and balance. There are, however, many other shapes the house could be and each shape sets up its own internal resonances, depending on how that shape affects the flow of energy – both magnetic and universal.

- **Rectangle** A rectangular shape is fine as long as the proportions are balanced; the length of the plot should be in proportion to the width. The length should never exceed twice the width.

- **Polygon** This shape can cause mental tension and insecurity. Any shape with more than four sides is not balanced according to the universal principles of Vaastu.

- **Triangle** This house shape is also unbalanced and liable to cause the occupants to enter into unnecessary civil disputes and legal actions that will cost them dearly in the long term. This is an unstable house shape and should be avoided.

Houses are often changed or extended and we need to be aware of how extensions affect us.

- **Circular/odd** Any shape which isn't regular will cause the occupants to have problems. A circular shape will cause the occupants to 'go round in circles' constantly.

Of course, what we start out with in terms of house shape may not be what we end up with. Here in the West we have a propensity for building on extensions to our dwellings. Perhaps it is the shortage of space or the reluctance to move to a bigger house. But whenever we need more room we build one on – and that can cause the occupants problems if the direction in which they build is not checked carefully.

- **South** Extensions built on the south can cause the occupants to lose money. This isn't an auspicious direction to project into. The south needs to be left clear and spacious and not cluttered with new buildings.
- **North** If you've got to build on then try to extend northwards. This really is the best direction and can benefit the occupants quite well since both wealth and health are said to increase as the building pushes into the north.
- **East** Building on to the east is said to increase the owner's fame and reputation.

- **West** Extending out into the west is said to seriously diminish the wealth of the occupant.
- **South-west** This can cause seemingly insurmountable problems. The problems may not exist, but building into the south-west causes despair and a reluctance to face facts.
- **South-east** Building into the south-east is said to increase the likelihood of fires in the building and is also reputedly said to attract burglars.
- **North-east** This is a good direction as it not only benefits health but also increases wealth and career.
- **North-west** This direction can lead to a loss of fortunes as well as a general impatience and restlessness. Money will be spent on worthless projects that can never come to fruition.

All of these principles also apply if you extend your property rather than just the house. If you add to your garden or extend fences out into neighbouring properties you need to check the directions carefully before doing so. Any extensions to the basic 'good' square of the house or the overall plot of land are to be viewed as the same thing.

Roads

To get to our houses we need a network of roads. To arrive at the front door we need only one road to take us to our drive. The direction from which we arrive at our house can benefit us in different ways.

- **North** A north road is said to increase our health.
- **South** A south road is said to increase our success.
- **West** A west road is said to increase our fame.
- **East** An east road is said to increase our wealth.

Two roads

If we have two roads converging or passing close to our property there are various combinations of influences depending on the directions.

- **North and east** Good for health, wealth and a peaceful life.
- **South and west** Said to be very good if you want to earn lots of money.
- **North and west** Good for success and prosperity.
- **South and east** Said to enhance relationships and allow women to find peace.

Three or four roads

If you are fortunate – according to Vaastu principles – to have three or four roads leading to your door, you are said to benefit from the energy of all three or four directions, bringing you peace, success, health and prosperity. A site near four roads is best, but obviously it isn't something we have any choice in – that's for the town planners.

Angle of approach

The road needs to approach the house directly from the compass direction, not acutely or at an angle because that does not enhance the flow of energy. The first diagram on the right shows this approach.

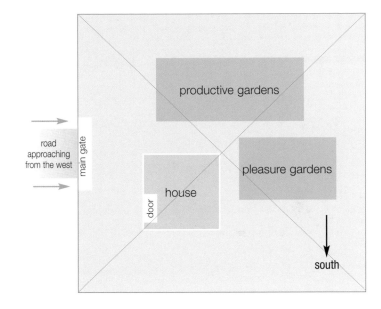

A direct approach road

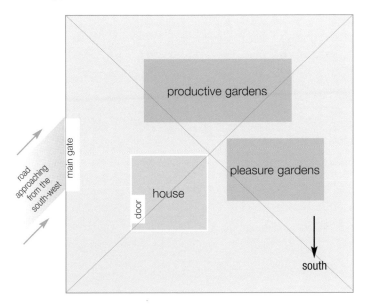

An oblique approach road

If the road approaches at an oblique angle it is known as *veedhi shoola* (*veedhi* means 'street' and *shoola* means 'touching'). Depending on which compass direction it is coming from, this brings either benefits or disadvantages.

- **North-east** This is said to bring health, wealth and, generally, happiness.
- **North-west** This direction is said not to be auspicious. It is believed to bring legal problems and a general feeling that all is not well – restlessness and fear.
- **South-west** This is another 'bad' direction in that it is said to bring a loss of fortune and prestige.
- **South-east** This direction is said to bring ill health and legal problems.

You will see that on the whole having a road approach at an oblique angle isn't a good idea. Vaastu depends on balance and harmony – all straight lines and good 'squares'. Introducing an oblique angle is said to interfere with the energy flow and cause problems.

Ground levels

It was suggested earlier that it is a good idea to ensure that the east and north parts of your plot are at a lower level than the south and west if you can't align your house along a north/south axis. Otherwise, however, having the ground higher in the north and east is better than the other way round. Bear in mind that if rainwater runs off well, by having these higher ground areas you will benefit, but if it doesn't your house may flood. The rules of Vaastu are not set in stone. You have to adjust things to suit your local weather variations and conditions.

Ground levels outside the plot

If there are hills to the west and south of your property this is said to be 'good' and to bring health and wealth to all the occupants of the house. But depression in the south or west is said to bring loss of wealth and loss of health. Hills in the north and east are said to be good for prosperity and fame. And similarly depressions in the ground are said to bring about a loss of prosperity and fame.

Ground levels within the boundaries of the plot

Generally the ground is considered 'good' if it is level or gently sloping. If there are sudden depressions or sunken areas these may bring about misfortune, depending on where they are. If they happen to be in the north or east they are considered to be all right and bring about good health and prosperity. If they are in the north-east then they bring about both. The other directions have the following influences:

- **South-east** – bad for women and all male children
- **South-west** – loss of health and money
- **North-west** – bring about personal enemies
- **West** – loss of fame and wealth
- **South** – splits in family relationships and arguments

Wells and springs

Not many of us are lucky enough to have a well or a spring in the garden, but if you do then where it is placed will have certain benefits or disadvantages. Having water in the garden is said, generally, to be beneficial, especially if the water is flowing. Obviously, as we have seen, certain directions are 'good' while others are 'bad'.

Water centrally placed in any of the four cardinal points of the compass – north/south/east/west – is said to be 'good' and to bring wealth, health, happiness and success. The siting of the water has to be in good proportion to the house and to be in balance and harmony – see the diagram.

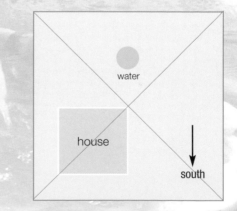

Water in a good position and well placed

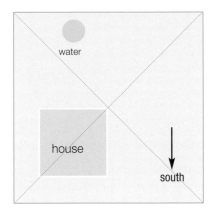

Water in a good position but badly placed

If the water is offset or obliquely placed it is said to be generally 'bad' and should be avoided if possible.

- **South-east** Water here is said to be harmful to women and children.

- **South-west** Water here is said to result in a loss of wealth as well as causing accidents.

- **North-east** In this direction water is said to cause ill health.

- **North-west** Here water is said to improve the finances of the family and help family members gain promotion. This is the only oblique direction for water that is considered to be good.

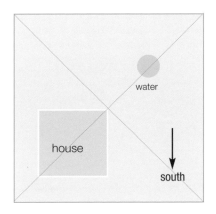

Water 'badly' placed in the north-east

Having water in the garden in considered essential to Vaastu.

- **Centrally placed water sources** Any wells or springs occurring directly in the centre of the plot are said to bring about hardship and insurmountable problems.

The five elements

Before we can consider the main house we need to have an understanding of the five-element theory of Indian philosophy. The five elements are known as the *panchabhutas*. They are:

Aakasha – Space

This element incorporates all the cosmic energies such as gravitational forces, magnetic fields and heat and light waves. Its main characteristic is known as *shabd*, which could be translated as 'sound'.

Vaayu – Air

This element is the atmosphere around us, what we breath and what transmits *prana* – universal breath. Its main characteristic is *sparsh* – touch.

Agni – Fire

This element represents the heat and light of fires, lightning and volcanoes, as well as the heat of fevers, energy, passion and vigour. Its main characteristic is *roop* – form.

Jala – Water

This element represents everything liquid – rain, rivers, the sea, as well as steam and clouds. It also represents all living plant material and its main characteristic is *ras* – taste.

Bhumi – Earth

This element represents all solid matter, as well as everything we stand on – the Earth itself. It is also the element of quality – *gun*.

These five elements are very important to Vaastu and we shall return to them several times later on in the book. Each of the elements is said to 'control' a part of the house, as well as contributing to the parts of the human body: we are all a unique blend or mixture of these five elements.

In Vaastu, the selection of a site and the way the house is built with reference to proportion and size are important factors. The house should radiate positive energy, depending on its shape, size, location and direction. The five elements play an important part in this. If any area of your home is too large – and thus has too much of any one element – it will affect you adversely, according to your *jyotish* (astrological alignment) – see page 86.

The five elements are grouped around your home according to their traditional locations:

- **North to west** – air
- **North to east** – water
- **East to south** – fire
- **South to west** – earth
- **Central** – space

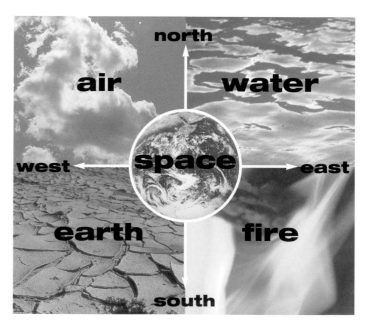

The location of the five elements

You can see from the diagram that any area that is overly large or extended outwards will upset the balance of the five elements – and balance is what Vaastu is all about. Your house is divided into this five-element pattern; so too is every room. Each room needs to carry the right proportions and the right shape. If you have 'L'-shaped rooms you have extended one of these five elements and this will affect you adversely.

The right locations for the rooms

You can also begin to see why, according to Vaastu principles, certain rooms should be located in certain areas of the house. For example, Vaastu dictates that the kitchen should always be located in the south-east corner of the home. This is the region of fire. And fire is what is needed in a kitchen. Whereas the main bedroom should be located in the south-west corner to benefit from the element of earth.

The space element

The central portion of the home is reserved for the element of space – the cosmic element. In traditional Vaastu the centre of the home is reserved for the pooja room – the meditation or prayer room. This is regarded as the most important room in the whole house, so we will have a look at it in some depth.

The pooja room

If you look at a ground plan of your house, you can overlay the compass points on it and then see how the five elements correspond. The part between the north and west is the air element area; between the west and south is the earth area; between the south and east is the fire area; between the east and north is the water area. The very centre of your home is governed by the element known as space or *prana*. *Prana* is universal energy or cosmic breath. It is the vital force that energizes us and keeps us alive. You may like to think of it as soul or spirit, although such Western terms can be misleading. Or you may like to

consider the Chinese equivalent – *chi*. As we breathe in and out we are not only replacing our air supply but also replenishing our supply of *prana*. Since *prana* occupies the central portion of our home, we can see why it is so important to locate the pooja room there. The pooja room needs to benefit from universal energy if it is to function correctly as our focus on higher or more spiritual matters.

It is traditional to overlay a diagrammatic picture of the human body on to the ground plan. The head resides in the water element in the north-east. The feet reside in the south-west, the earth element, to keep us grounded. Our left side is in the south-east – fire – and our right side in the north-west – air. The heart, lungs and centre of our being reside in the *prana* centre of our home – the pooja room. Thus as human beings we embody the five elements, just as our home does.

There is an old Hindu saying:

If you are not for yourself, who are you for?
If you are for yourself, what are you for?
And if not now, when?

The pooja room is for you. It is your private sanctuary – and also for your family of course; but it is a room dedicated to the people in the house. It is dedicated to your pursuit of something bigger in this life. Bigger than your career. Bigger than money or fame or success. All these things are for this life. They are transitory and impermanent. They will not last. The pooja room is dedicated to something that will last. Something that will return again and again – according to Hindu philosophy – to be reborn countless times until we get it 'right'. If not now, when? The pooja room is for those who have decided that now means 'now'. This is the time to dedicate a part of our lives to something bigger, something more important. It is a room in which to begin the search for peace and true fulfilment. Without a pooja room the home is just a dwelling. With a pooja room the home is more – a temple, a shrine, a refuge and an embarkation point to a richer more spiritual life.

One of the most important aspects of the pooja room is the altar. The mystical link between heaven and earth is established; it is a clear and visible focus on matters other than the mundane. The altar gives us meaning in our ordinary, everyday lives and serves to remind us that we are more than mere flesh and blood; that we are as much creatures of the universe as the angels and spirits themselves.

We all have altars

For some people the idea of an altar is new and unusual. But if you look around your home you will probably find that you have already built many altars without realizing it. Look at the mantelpiece above your fireplace. What have you got there? Photos of loved ones? Mementoes? A mirror? A picture? Art? The chances are that it is already well on the way to being an altar.

The same goes for the bedroom. Most of us have some sort of dressing table. It usually has a mirror with a collection of bottles, perfumes, powders, brushes, combs, tissues, the odd photo, scarves, ties, jewellery – that sort of thing. We have an innate need to build altars. Visit the bathroom and see if you haven't done the same here. Perhaps you keep it all out of sight in a cabinet, but open it and the altar design is there – the bottles, the canisters, the razors and cotton buds. They all serve as sacred objects to us.

We even carry around portable altars. Open your purse or wallet or handbag. In there are all the sacred relics you feel devastated without – the filofax, the mobile phone, the lighter, money, lucky charms, diaries, pens, matches, lipstick, keys. We carry our altar with us always. Building a special altar with a true meaning doesn't imply change. It merely signifies that we consciously build it, instead of doing so in the unconscious way that we do now.

The pooja altar

The altar is our sacred shrine to whatever belief system we choose to follow. Our shrine can be simple or complex, arranged to a fixed pattern or designed as part of an ongoing organic process. Whatever method we choose for building our altar, it must be done with a clear focus on the spiritual, the divinity within us. Here we will crystallize our inner dreams and aspirations; we will worship before the enormous power and force of the universe. Our shrine will provide us with a sacred and holy place within the very centre of our home – an intensely private and personal space.

The focus

Before you select statues or natural objects or holy relics you must have a mental picture of what your altar is going to represent. If you already subscribe to an organized religion, you may have iconic images that suit your belief system, such as a Holy Mary if you are a Roman Catholic or a statue of the Buddha if you are one of his followers. But if you embrace a belief system more closely related to the natural world, one which you follow alone or with a few friends, you need to decide which objects or mementoes represent your approach to spirituality. And it must be intensely personal. It doesn't matter what the current

...whatever method we choose to build our altar, it must be done with a clear focus on the spiritual...

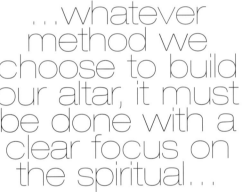

fashion or trend is, you must feel comfortable with what you choose. You must focus carefully and closely on what spirituality means to you.

Choosing icons

Before you choose, you should consider what you will use your altar for. Will it be for personal meditation? Prayer and devotion? Quiet contemplation? Offering? There are no right and wrong answers. Perhaps a little of all of these things will be suitable for you. And remember that your altar is not fixed in either time or space. You can add to or subtract from your icons as you grow spiritually, or rearrange them to suit your mood and the different purposes for which you may use your altar.

Choose objects which mean something to you. Natural objects work best, if you don't have religious icons from an established religion. Feathers, wood, stones, a bowl of water, hand-carved statues, shells, crystals, natural fabrics such as silk or wool, beads, fruit, flowers and, of course, candles. When choosing objects, allow your heart to speak. Feel the objects. Are they right? Do they feel as if they contain the essence of the universe? Do they hum with the spirit that echoes your own?

Arranging your altar

Once you have chosen, you can arrange your objects. Again, follow your inner guide, let them speak for themselves as to where they feel best. Light a little incense and a candle. Allow natural light and scents to help you feel your way into the best arrangement. Sit quietly and let the objects settle and talk to you. If they seem wrong, they probably are – move them around until you feel happy with the arrangement. Add and subtract until the altar feels right for whatever purpose you have intended.

Try always to incorporate the four Hindu elements of air, water, earth and fire – incense burning, a bowl of natural spring water, a stone or a clay object, and a candle to represent fire. The fifth element – *prana* or space – is you of course. Lay the objects out according to the correct compass directions of the five elements, with space in the middle, fire in the south-east, air in the north-west, water in the north-east and earth in the south-west.

Using the pooja room

You can use your pooja room alone for meditation or prayer or just as a safe haven to get away from the rest of the world. If you share the pooja room with the rest of the family it is worth laying down some ground rules to stop it becoming just another sitting room. Make sure that shoes are removed and that everyone appreciates the need for peace and quiet. If

conversation is to go on, then make sure it is *satsang* – talk about spiritual issues – and not just chitchat.

Other rooms in your home

If we imagine energy entering our home from our front door, located along the south-west wall, into our earth area, we can see how the rooms should be arranged. The energy enters the ground floor and wakes us in our bedroom on the first floor in the earth area (though don't forget that most Indian homes are built on one floor, with the bedroom being on the ground floor). The earth energy is heavy and rich with life. It is dense and just what we need to get us through the day – invigorating and strong. We, and the energy, enter the south-east region of fire where we cook and eat breakfast.

Next the energy takes us into the north-east area of water where we carry out our ablutions – this is the location for the bathroom. The energy then spirals into the north-west area of air – representing mental activity – where we work and earn our living (unless, of course, we have to go out to work).

Lastly the energy spirals into the central area of space. This energy is now light and spiritual. Here we enter the pooja room where we turn our thoughts to higher things. We meditate before retiring for the night, when we go back to the earth room again. The way in which the energy moves is also a metaphor for the way the energy moves through our life.

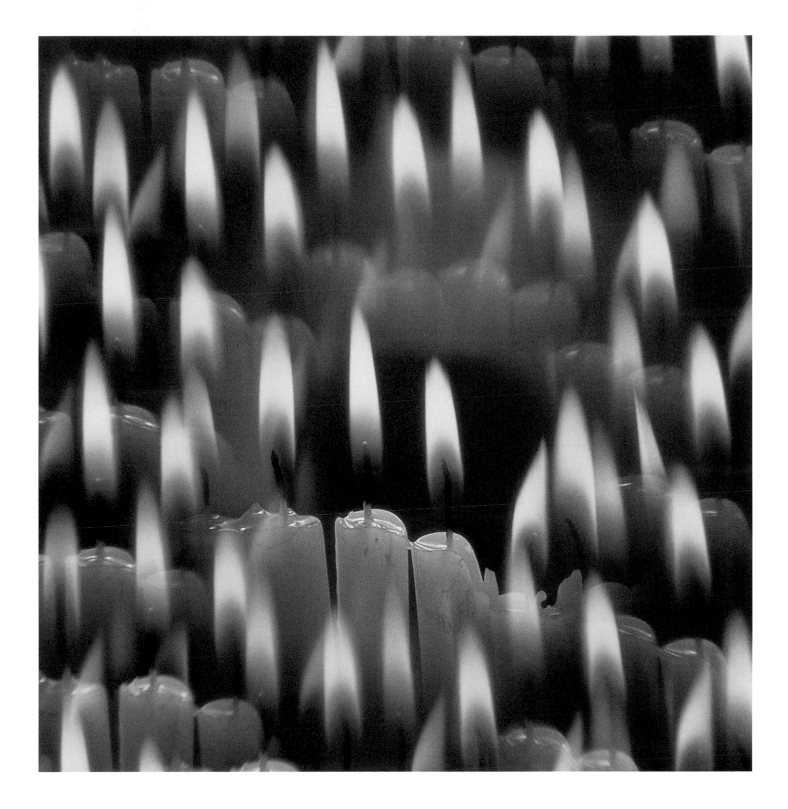

The metaphor of life

We are born of earth, heavy with new life. We spend time eating and growing in the fire areas of childhood and teens. The energy takes us into the water areas of our life, where we travel and expand our knowledge. We enter the air areas of middle age where we earn our living, think, philosophize and work. Lastly the energy takes us into the space of spiritual dimensions as we grow older, before returning us to be reborn in the earth once again, an earth heavy with sexual and material energy.

Understanding Vaastu

If we understand the way energy moves from heavy to light in a spiral, anticlockwise, and how each of the areas of the five elements shapes our lives, we can perceive much about the way Vaastu works, without needing lists of principles or charts or diagrams. Following a book is fine, but understanding Vaastu is better. If I tell you, you will remember for a day. If I show you, you will remember for a week. But if you do it for yourself, you will remember it always.

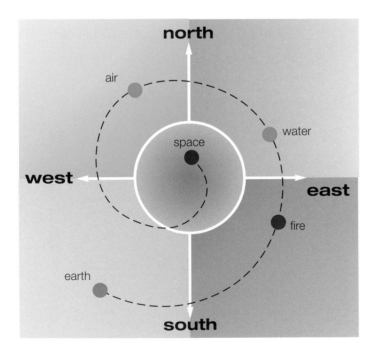

The spiral of energy from earth to space

This left-hand spiral of energy is worth remembering since it affects all aspects of Vaastu. The key points are:

- Energy flows in a spiral.
- Energy flows in an anticlockwise direction.
- Energy gets lighter as it nears the centre.
- Energy gets faster as it nears the centre.
- Energy undergoes a transformation as it spirals from the earth to the space element through fire, water and air.

All energy moves. All energy sustains life. All energy is *prana* – universal breath. Anything without energy is *pradhana* – primary matter. Something is either alive or not. If it is alive, it is filled with energy. If it is not alive, it has no energy. Energy cannot be destroyed but it can leave something and render it *pradhana* – inert. Although the energy cannot be destroyed, it can be impeded, speeded up, stagnated, corrupted or even diverted. When you practise Vaastu you are allowing energy to flow well, to enhance its progress. You are not trying to transform it – it will do that itself. You are merely providing the best routes, the most auspicious locations, the right sort of proportions and harmony.

The Vaastu *purusha*

If we take our ground plan as a square – according to vedic tradition – we can divide that square into a grid of 64 smaller squares. Each of these smaller squares becomes an entity in itself.

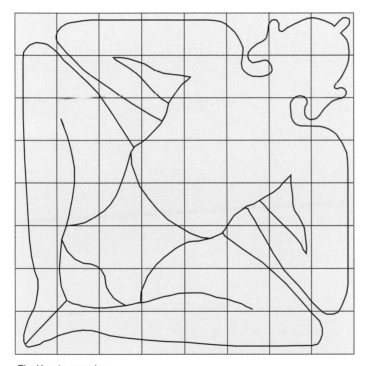

The Vaastu purusha

Overlaid on these 64 squares, traditionally, was the outline of the human figure. This is the Vaastu *purusha* – the divine form.

Traditionally the human form is always arranged so that the head is in the north-east and the feet together in the south-west. But according to your *jyotish* – astrological alignment – this human form can be rotated to suit your own needs. We will examine this

in more detail in Chapter 5. The *purusha* is a human representation of perfect balance and harmony. This figure is exactly right, according to the *Vedas*. It is neither too tall nor too fat nor too thin nor too short. It perfectly fits into a square house or room. You can see that if the room was rectangular the *purusha* wouldn't fit so well. Imagine the *purusha* as yourself. If you try to squeeze yourself into a shape that doesn't fit, you will feel uncomfortable. Imagine that each room in your house contains the *purusha* and ask yourself:

- Do I fit this room well?
- Do I feel squeezed?
- Do I feel uncomfortable in this room?
- Is this room adhering to the basic principles of the *purusha*?

Depending on your answers, you will already see what changes you might have to make to allow the *purusha* – your shadow soul, if you like – to fit more comfortably. Rectangular rooms should be made more square: you can do this with room dividers – in effect, turning a rectangular room into two smaller rooms, both square. If the room is 'L'-shaped you can do the same thing with room dividers. The *purusha* can be made smaller but should not be distorted.

This chapter has outlined the basic principles of Vaastu according to traditional vedic lore. As we saw earlier, there are three parts to Vaastu – *shastra*, *ayurveda* and *jyotish* (later, we shall look at a fourth part – practical Vaastu).

Now that we have covered the basic principles of the building plot – *shastra* – in the next chapter we can look at what happens to the occupants of the house – *ayurveda*.

ayurveda
the way
we live

According to traditional vedic wisdom, the way you live is as important in combating illness as treating any disease you suffer from.

This may not come as a surprise, knowing what we do these days about a holistic approach to health, but you must remember that this approach has been in use in India for some eight thousand years. The ancient Sanskrit literature talks about living conditions as being very important to health. If we get the environment wrong our internal system will be uneasy and cause us digestive, reproductive and nervous problems. If we get it right we are vitalized, energized and our immune system strengthened and more able to ward off illness.

In India they don't see disease as something that attacks us from the outside but more as something that we allow to penetrate our defences by wrong living. If we live in the right way in terms of diet, housing, lifestyle, spiritual faith and exercise, then we are that much stronger and more able to repel any attack from outside. First, we must understand ourselves according to the basic principles of ayurvedic medicine.

Health and *ayurveda*

Ayurveda is the ancient treatise that deals with health. This doesn't just mean the health of ancients living at the dawn of time: it speaks very personally to each of us individually today. It helps us to find out which type of person we are – there are three distinct types – so that our diet and way of living can be adjusted accordingly. This makes sense. If we are of a fiery nature, ill-tempered and angry, for instance, it would not suit us to live in the same environment or under the same conditions as someone calmer, more intellectual and more passive. And then again, perhaps we are fearful, greedy, creative, caring, emotional, athletic and so on. We need to know which type we are so that we can make the appropriate adjustments.

The three types

There are three basic types of people – *dosha* – in *ayurveda*: these are *vata*, *pitta* and *kapha*. Then there are the various combinations of these, because people are rarely just of one type. Before we look at these, we must realize that we probably have a basic type – *prakruti* – and a current or recent type – *vikruti*. For instance, you might be *vata* but recently have been suffering a bout of illness or depression which has altered your state to that of *kapha*. Before you could revert to true type, the *kapha* would have to be treated. This would be done by diet, exercise or changing the Vaastu of your home to implement a more beneficial energy flow and greater harmony.

Basic energies

Before you read about the three *dosha* it might be useful to look at how these three types have evolved from an understanding of the five elements.

Vata is the element of air combined with space – *prana* (universal breath or cosmic energy). It is representative of change and movement, like the wind that is its principal aspect. *Pitta* is a combination of fire and water. It is representative of conversion and transformation, like the Sun which is its principal aspect. *Kapha* is a combination of water

and earth and is representative of cohesion and unity, like the Moon which is its principal aspect.

- *Vata* types are said to be changeable and active personalities subject to stress.
- *Pitta* types are fiery and like to make changes, to motivate and to be in charge. They are prone to suffer from anger and high blood pressure.
- *Kapha* types are calmer, more sedate and slower moving. They are intuitive, sensitive and like to pace themselves. They may suffer from depression and a fear of change.

Remember also that your body may be of one type, while your mind is another type completely. Let's look at how we determine which type we are, what that means, what illnesses we might be prone to and how we should manage our diet and lifestyle.

Finding your *dosha*

To understand what your *dosha* is you need to answer a few questions. This isn't a test, nor is it an exam with a prize or qualification. There is no spiritual gain to be had from pretending to be one type when you are really another type. There is no better or worse type. Each of the three *dosha* has certain benefits and certain disadvantages.

The characteristics of each type are listed in the chart below. Tick the boxes as appropriate. Try to answer as honestly as possible and if you get stuck or aren't sure what to answer then ask a friend or partner as they may know you better than you think, or indeed know yourself.

Bear in mind that we are trying to find out both your basic type – *prakruti* – and your current or recent type – *vikruti*. Mark the appropriate boxes with a tick if this is your general constitution and with a cross if this is your current constitution.

You can see from this that you could have a possible 'top' score of 28 for any one category. Not that I should imagine there is anyone who would score such a total. And if they did, they would be seriously out of balance. The chances are you will score, on average, more for one category than another. It might only be slightly more but that is enough to determine which type you are. Ideally we should all be a good blend of all three.

	Vata	general	current	*Pitta*	general	current	*Kapha*	general	current
1. **Movement**	quick	❑	❑	average	❑	❑	slow	❑	❑
2. **Body frame**	light/slender	❑	❑	medium	❑	❑	heavy/solid	❑	❑
3. **Complexion**	dark	❑	❑	sensitive	❑	❑	medium	❑	❑
4. **Elimination**	constipated	❑	❑	loose	❑	❑	average	❑	❑
5. **Emotions**	anxious	❑	❑	buoyant	❑	❑	needy	❑	❑
6. **Eye size**	small	❑	❑	medium	❑	❑	large	❑	❑
7. **Eye type**	brown	❑	❑	blue/grey	❑	❑	green	❑	❑
8. **Gums**	receding	❑	❑	bleed easily	❑	❑	strong/good	❑	❑
9. **Hair quality**	average	❑	❑	thin/grey	❑	❑	thick	❑	❑
10. **Hair type**	fine	❑	❑	soft	❑	❑	coarse	❑	❑
11. **Height**	very short/tall	❑	❑	medium	❑	❑	short/tall	❑	❑
12. **Lifestyle**	changeable	❑	❑	busy	❑	❑	steady	❑	❑
13. **Memory**	good	❑	❑	average	❑	❑	good long term	❑	❑
14. **Mental type**	creative	❑	❑	analytical	❑	❑	calm	❑	❑
15. **Moods**	changeable	❑	❑	predictable	❑	❑	steady	❑	❑
16. **Muscle type**	thin/wiry	❑	❑	medium	❑	❑	muscular	❑	❑
17. **Skin**	dry/cold	❑	❑	soft/warm	❑	❑	moist/cool	❑	❑
18. **Sleep**	light	❑	❑	sound	❑	❑	deep	❑	❑
19. **Speech**	quick	❑	❑	precise	❑	❑	slow	❑	❑
20. **Stamina**	low	❑	❑	average	❑	❑	high	❑	❑
21. **Stress factors**	excitable	❑	❑	irritated easily	❑	❑	calm	❑	❑
22. **Sweating**	rarely	❑	❑	frequently	❑	❑	medium	❑	❑
23. **Teeth**	protruding	❑	❑	yellowish	❑	❑	white	❑	❑
24. **Teeth size**	small	❑	❑	average	❑	❑	large	❑	❑
25. **Temperature**	aversion to cold	❑	❑	aversion to heat	❑	❑	aversion to damp	❑	❑
26. **Weight**	under average (thin)	❑	❑	average	❑	❑	above average (fat)	❑	❑
27. **Work**	creative	❑	❑	academic	❑	❑	people orientated	❑	❑
Pulse when resting									
28. **Men**	above 75	❑	❑	65–75	❑	❑	under 65	❑	❑
29. **Women**	above 85	❑	❑	75–85	❑	❑	under 75	❑	❑
Totals									

First we shall look at the three types of *dosha*, but as general types, not current types. Current types may need to be rectified if they are substantially different from the general type – it indicates a body out of harmony and balance. This balance will need to be restored first before you can equate the general type with Vaastu.

Vata

Vata is produced by combining the two elements of space and air. Energy gets faster as it moves towards space. *Vata* people move fast. They think fast. They make quick decisions and they talk fast.

Vata people are usually thin people who don't put on weight easily. They are often restless and of a nervous disposition. They are likely to be active and busy. Because they are thin they tend to feel the cold more easily than others. They have little in the way of reserves and tend to exhaust themselves too much. They often find it hard to relax and overcommit themselves. Because they are very mentally active they may find it hard to sleep or switch off. Generally their health will be average to good, although they are found to suffer from arthritis and nervous disorders. If they have prolonged bouts of ill health it is usually of depression and fearfulness.

They have delicate stomachs and any nervousness will instantly put them off their food. They can suffer from poor

appetites generally and are picky eaters. Because they eat little they can suffer from constipation.

They need to eat regularly and avoid all fried foods. Although vegetables are recommended for everyone, *vata* types also need to keep up their intake of meat and fish as it helps ground them and build up their constitution.

They should take a little exercise – not too strenuous – and keep up a regular regime of working out so that they build up their strength. Exercising will help them keep their minds rested. They need to establish routines in everything they do to avoid jumping from one thing to another without allowing themselves to rest in between. Basically they are nervous people who suffer from anxiety and should lead quiet, calm lives if they want to avoid nervous disorders.

Vata types need to surround themselves with pastel colours to soothe their overactive minds. The earthy colours of ochre, browns and yellows have a soothing influence. They need colours that are warm, solid and reliable.

Vata people benefit from regular massages, especially of the lower back where they tend to build up tension. They also need their feet and hands massaged as they suffer from poor circulation, particularly in cold weather which they have an aversion to. *Vata* people also benefit from meditation as it helps soothe and calm their overdynamic minds.

Pitta

Pitta is produced by combining the two elements of fire and water – an interesting combination since it can be either very productive (fire heats water to cook) or very destructive (water puts out the internal fires). But whatever way it manifests itself, the *pitta* type is usually well balanced. They may be seen as average in all they do, but we would soon be lost without *pitta* types. *Vata* is the creative energy, but *pitta* is the engineer and the developer. *Kapha*, if you were wondering, is the one who sees the project along on a day-to-day basis.

Pitta types are intense and fiery but they do like to be of use – the cooking combination of water and fire. They are sensitive to the sun and burn easily – in more ways than one. They like to be cool, both in temperature and in their attitude. They prefer northern latitudes and the colder the climate, the more they like it. They sweat too much in hot moist climates so they never feel really comfortable there. They may claim to love the sun but deep down they are more comfortable in a cooler region.

Vata people are creative as long as they receive sufficient training in a skill or craft. They need gentle exercise – yoga is very good for them, as are swimming and walking – and they should avoid foods which give high energy, instant hits such as sugar and chocolate bars, as this type of energy isn't very good for the *vata* type. What they need is good food that is well cooked and nourishing – lots of warming soups, stews, fresh baked bread and nursery puddings. They need to be kept warm, and comforted and looked after. They may appear to be independent and self-reliant but at heart they are children and need to be nurtured. They don't recover quickly from setbacks and will give up easily if faced with too many obstacles.

They are very kind people, just so long as you ask them for help because they won't volunteer it. They have a certain reserve which stops them from pushing themselves forward and they don't like to seem pushy.

They like to be challenged, especially in their work. They can't stand to be idle or bored. They can be impatient and sometimes need to learn tact and self-control. They are able to set a cracking good pace at whatever task they take on. They have good stamina and strength but often don't know when to stop and can physically wear themselves out. They like to make their living using their wits and sharp brains rather than their hands but they aren't averse to plain hard work if it's needed.

They are people whose feathers ruffle easily and they need to be soothed. Everything about them is

like order and stability. Colourwise they need to be soothed – blues, greens and violets will do this for them. All cool colours, all pastel shades are good. Lots of white in their furnishings and decor will enhance the cooling effect and soothe their jagged nerves. They need to come home to order and space, cool colours and no clutter. Clutter will make them feel irritable and 'hot'.

Pitta types like to be challenged in all things, so any exercise they take up should include this essential element: running, competitive sports, martial arts, team games are all good as the element of winning is important to them. The *pitta* nature is always to overdo things so exercise shouldn't become an obsession, which it sometimes can. Moderation in all things should be their motto. Sport should be engaged in for its enjoyment value but the *pitta* type will always go for the winning rather than the pleasure. This is also true in their relationships, where they like to be in control and in charge.

Kapha

Kapha types are formed by combining the two elements of water and earth. The water can feed the earth to bring forth new growth, but if there is too much water the earth may turn to mud. *Kapha* people are stocky and agricultural. They tend to run to fat if they don't watch what they eat. They need to keep active and move a lot; though they are naturally hard-working they can still put on weight. They sometimes lack motivation and, although busy, can become lazy.

slightly inflamed much of the time. This applies to their digestive system as much as anything and they must avoid hot, spicy foods at all times. They'd be better off eating a vegetarian diet: *ayurveda* recommends vegetarianism for most people, but for the *pitta* type it is essential. They should avoid dairy products and eggs too. If they do want to eat meat they should stick to very lean white meat that has been raised by organic and free-range methods. If they ever feel the fire is burning them up and they are becoming unstable then a diet of rice and plain water will cool them down and soothe their inflamed digestive system. All their health problems will relate to this inflammation and they should pay particular attention to their diet as they are more susceptible to dietary problems than the other types.

Pitta people don't take to change too easily and need routine and conformity. They

They are emotional people who use food as an outlet for suppressed emotions. They can be stubborn and refuse to see other people's point of view at times and they do tend to be very conservative, disliking change or innovation. They are very traditional and reserved, even shy at times. They like to acquire possessions since they feel that a well-stocked larder or a healthy bank account will protect them from emotional ravages.

Kapha people are caring and protective, especially of their families. They genuinely worry about their offspring and partners and can seem fussy and overprotective at times. Because they dislike feeling cold or damp they overheat their homes, which leads them to feel even more sluggish and lazy. A good therapy for *kapha* types is lots of fresh air and a change of scenery from time to time to stop them becoming bogged down in all the self-generated mud.

Kapha people are slow thinkers, taking a long time to make decisions. This isn't indecisiveness but a result of a methodical, logical mind that likes to weight the facts and consider the pros and cons before rushing into anything. You won't hurry a *kapha* type so it's best to wait: what they come up with will invariably turn out to be the right decision, albeit the one which errs on the side of caution. They don't like to gamble or take risks.

In terms of diet they should avoid fatty foods. They should eat meat in strict moderation. The best foods for them are lots of vegetables, which should ideally be cooked. Raw food should be avoided. They should lay off the sugar and any additives or sweeteners. They need a plain, unrefined diet and should even avoid wheat products.

Best colours for *kapha* types

are the warm ones – reds, oranges, pinks and Mediterranean colours. They need warmth, brightness and stimulation. In both their clothing and their decor they need colours that will stimulate them and invigorate them.

Kapha people are basically sleepy and need to be woken up by fresh air, forceful massage, lots of exercise, bright colours and plenty of mental challenges. All of these they will resist as they like to be indulgent and lazy. Aerobics is good exercise for them but they need to be disciplined about it. They will find any excuse not to work out or take care of themselves physically. However, they really do benefit from vigorous exercise and should take up running, swimming, weight-lifting or dancing.

Dual *dosha*

When you filled in the questionnaire you probably scored more 'points' for one type than for the other two. If, however, you had an equal score for two types – and these were more than the other one – then you may well be a combination of two *dosha*. This means that instead of a combination of two elements you might well be a mixture of three or even four elements. This isn't a bad thing, it merely takes a little more understanding to see who you really are. It might also mean that you experience seasonal changes, where you might feel fine in the summer, say, but wretched in the winter. This is because one of the elements is trying to dominate the others or is pulled out of harmony by the close relationship of the others.

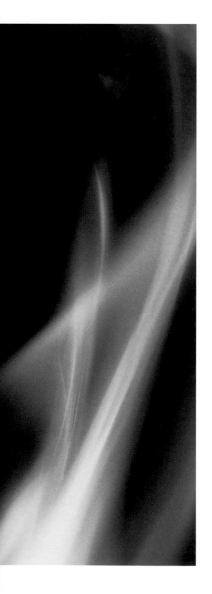

Vata/pitta

Here we have four elements competing – space, air, fire and water. You should consider yourself *vata* in the winter and *pitta* in the summer (winter includes autumn and summer includes spring). The anger and irritability of the *pitta* may be a result of the fearfulness of the *vata* so you need to watch and control your temper as you are likely to sound off without realizing it and cause harm by being unduly outspoken. *Vata/pitta* types can be mentally very bright indeed, which may sometimes cause them to lose contact with people – they are so brainy and creative that they lose the common touch and become reclusive or withdrawn.

This type can also be very unpredictable – just when you think you know what they will do, they act completely out of character and surprise you indeed. They make excellent communicators, just so long as they learn to pitch their presentations at the audience and not over their heads.

They are excitable people who get fired up easily and are ready for new projects. They hate daily routine and conformity. They don't

like to be judged, ordered, tidied up or straightened out. They are fiercely independent and very self-assured. They don't tolerate fools around them and can be very demanding to work for.

To achieve balance and harmony they need to watch their diet. They should eat what is in season because this will suit whichever of the two types is dominating, according to the season.

You may find that if you are this combination of *dosha*, then your mind may be *vata* and your body *pitta*, or the other way round. Thus you can react in one way as *vata* and in another as *pitta*. This helps you understand yourself and where you are coming from. It might be that your intellectual processes are governed by one type and your emotional responses by the other. Again, if you know which is which then it is easier to understand yourself better.

Pitta/kapha

The *pitta/kapha* combination is formed by three elements – fire, water and earth. But it is double water which usually gives rise to a very emotional person indeed. The fire is extinguished and the earth damp and muddy. You need to assume you are *pitta* in the summer and spring, and *kapha* in the winter and autumn. You need lots of hot, spicy food to dry out all that water. Avoid watery foods such as salads and raw food and make sure you keep warm and eat often.

Pitta/kapha types can be very good at carrying out research as they have sharp, intellectual minds with a dogged determination that allows them to be relentless in their pursuit of facts and evidence. They can be very variable in mood and may fluctuate from immense calm to sudden bouts of irrational anger. They may suffer from a mild form of manic depression as a result of this. It also makes their personal relationships quite difficult since partners never know where they stand with them.

They are generally quite steady, slow people who work well and hard. They can be prone to a certain reluctance to take on new projects, but once involved they see things through to the end.

Vata/kapha

This combination is made up of the four elements of space, air, water and earth. Notice which is missing? Yes, fire. This type can be solid and dependable, reliable and hard-working, but lacking somewhat in motivation, spark and dynamism. They need to consider themselves as *vata* in the autumn and summer and during any dry windy conditions, and as *kapha* during the winter and spring and in damp cold weather.

The *vata/kapha* type is predominately cold and needs heat to generate any enthusiasm or excitement. Lots of hot, spicy food will do the trick, especially curries. This type also needs to avoid damp places and prefers dry clean heat to moist heat. They can sometimes be slow to speak but when they do, they seem to know what they are talking about. They like to catnap during the day and need somewhere warm to settle. They need security and protection around them if they are to feel really safe. They need nurturing and looking after.

Triple *dosha*

It is said that just occasionally, but very rarely, there is a triple *dosha* – someone who is equally split between all three types of *vata*, *pitta* and *kapha*. The triple *dosha* is so rare that it falls outside the brief of this book. If you think you might be one of these rare types then a visit to a fully qualified and experienced ayurvedic practitioner might be in order to help you fully understand the implications of such a type.

Ayurveda and Vaastu

Now that we have looked briefly at the concept of *ayurveda*, we can start to see how it might affect our practice of Vaastu.

We saw that each of the three types has a colour range that it feels at home with. These colours can be used for the interior decoration of the house.

Preferred colours

Vata	browns	yellows	ochre	light and earthy
Pitta	blues	greens	violet	natural and cool
Kapha	red	orange	pink	hot and dramatic

Pitta types need cool colours to keep them in check, to stop them rushing off at a tangent. They need balance and harmony in their colours, the colours of nature, to curb impatience and reduce irritability. If you are *pitta*, you can decorate your home with clean, cool, natural colours to soothe your soul and enhance your attention to spiritual matters.

Kapha types need hot colours to enliven them, to wake them up and to energize them. They need lots of the red end of the spectrum to counteract any symptoms of lethargy and laziness. *Kapha* is a low-energy type and needs lots of fire and heat to stop it falling asleep and missing opportunities. If you are *kapha* you need to be stimulated and excited, although you may well resist such activity. You can decorate your home with reddish colours and notice how invigorated you feel after only a very short time.

And it isn't only colours. The elements play an important part too. The chart on page 44, that we looked at earlier, showed where the elements fall in each house and room. If you now compare that with the diagram below, you will see how each type

Vata people need earthy, warm, gentle colours to encourage relaxation, enhance concentration and generally ground them. They need warmth to liven them up, but not hot colours which would overstimulate them. If you are *vata*, you can decorate your home in light, bright yellows and browns to help you focus your mind and keep your mental processes clear and fluid.

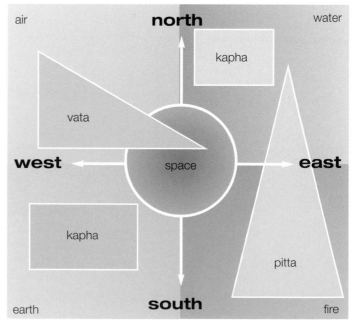

The location of the five elements with the three dosha

feels more comfortable with particular roles in the household duties and even in different rooms. The elements attributed to each *dosha* are:

- *Vata* – space and air
- *Pitta* – fire and water
- *Kapha* – water and earth

This equates to the mind, body and spirit trilogy of Western thinking:

- *Vata* – space and air: the lighter, spiritual energy that moves faster and is 'higher' and ascends to the cosmos.
- *Pitta* – fire and water: the mental facilities that affect thinking. The fire and water elements are also the basic requirements for a healthy mind, i.e. food and cleanliness.
- *Kapha* – water and earth: the body of the person. This is formed by a combination of slow-moving energy for strength and endurance, and faster water energy for vitality and life.

Compass directions are also important. Each of the three *dosha* needs to 'face' in their best directions:

- *Vata* – north-west
- *Pitta* – east
- *Kapha* – north-east and south-west

You can see from this that the *kapha* type can adapt more easily to change. They fit in almost anywhere, whereas *pitta* types, although accommodating both south and north within their element direction, only really feel at home in the east. *Vata* people prefer north and west.

The 'body' of *kapha* welcomes the energy, while the 'mind' of *pitta* transforms it and the 'soul' of *vata* utilizes it for spiritual growth.

Ideally, any home would contain all three types in order to be fully occupied and for the best use to be made of all its facilities. In traditional Indian culture no home would seem complete without children, the reason being that children increase the possible range of *dosha* types in the home and make it feel more complete.

The *dosha* cycles

Each of these three *dosha* also has a season when they feel 'best' and our living arrangements should accommodate this. It makes sense that if you feel good in the autumn and lousy in the summer, you should delay any important projects until you feel at your optimum. There are four seasons and therefore four 'states' for the dosha to be in:

- growing
- agitated
- declining
- resting

	Spring	Summer	Autumn	Winter
Vata	resting	growing	agitated	declining
Pitta	growing	agitated	declining	resting
Kapha	agitated	declining	resting	growing

You can see from this chart the natural cycle that each of these *dosha* goes through. They begin by growing, become agitated as they reach full fruition, decline as their production and energy fall off, and finally they rest for a season until they are ready to begin growth again.

It is helpful to be aware of your natural cycle. If you always feel drained and worn out in the autumn, it could be that you are *kapha* and should, by rights, be resting. Or perhaps you are always full of energy in the summer and ready for anything: it could be that you are *vata* and going through your growing stage. If you always feel bloated and irritated in the spring, it may be that you are *kapha* and feeling aggravated by all the growth you did in the winter.

both advocates of a natural way of being. Living in accord with the weather and the seasons is much harder in the West, where every action seems to be controlled by the clock. We get up when the clock tells us to rather than when we've had enough sleep. We travel to work in the dark in winter and return home again in the dark. We eat at set times rather than when we feel hungry.

If you know what cycle your own *dosha* is in, you may be able to treat yourself a little more gently. Get up when you are rested; exercise when you are in your growing stage; get out there and conquer the world when you are in your agitated stage; take things easier when you are in decline.

Each of the three *dosha* has not only a seasonal cycle but also a daily one, a yearly one (the seasonal one we've looked at) and a lifetime one.

Knowing the three *dosha* and the seasonal cycle they go through enables us to plan our lives better. Why decorate in the winter when you are *pitta* and should be resting? Wait until the spring when you feel full of energy and growth.

The dosha *cycles and relationships*

Knowing this cycle also helps us in our relationships. If two people are the same *dosha* it is easy to match each other's moods. But if they are different, it makes sense to try to understand the other person's cycle. One person may be all fired up and enthusiastic about a new project, while the other seems dull and listless. It could be that the latter is going through their resting stage just as the former is entering their growing stage. Or perhaps one feels quarrelsome and irritated by the other when they seem to be unenthusiastic: the first is agitated and the second is declining. Both partners will be more tolerant when they know what is happening.

Natural cycles

Vaastu is about choosing how and where we live. *Ayurveda* is about the way in which we live. The two go hand in hand. They are

The daily cycle

The daily cycle has four six-hour periods. The cycle follows the same formula as the seasonal cycle – growing, agitated, declining, resting. These periods roughly equate to our twenty-four hour day, although you may have to adjust them slightly. If you watch how you feel it will quickly become apparent where the cycle needs to be adjusted to suit yourself. These periods were originally set for Indian latitudes and as we move progressively north or west they change a little.

	Midnight–6 am	6 am–12 noon	12 noon–6 pm	6 pm–midnight
Vata	declining	resting	growing	agitated
Pitta	growing	agitated	declining	resting
Kapha	resting	growing	agitated	declining

You can see from this that *kapha* people – those who like lots of deep sleep – rest most between the hours of midnight and six in the morning. On the other hand, *vata* types – those who sleep fitfully and very lightly indeed – are actually better off spending the morning in bed catching up on the sleep they missed before midnight when they were going through their agitated phase. Perhaps we need to clarify exactly what the agitated phase is.

The agitated phase: Being agitated means that you have become full to the point of bursting. It is your most productive stage, the time when you think best, create new ideas, are full of talk and conversation, are fruitful with inspiration and creativity. Your agitated stage is when you are most restless, and also perhaps most quarrelsome, as if all those new ideas need an outlet and you feel stifled if you aren't allowed to pour them forth.

Your agitated stage is when you are most alive, most aware of the wonders of the world. This is the time when you should be out in the world, taking control of your life, being large and loud and dynamic. It is not a time to stay at home reading or doing the crossword. Some people find the agitated stage extremely disruptive, as if they have come into blossom but don't know what to do with it. They are heavy with expectation and anticipation, but life isn't offering them any outlet for all that creative energy.

The declining phase: This phase occurs when the outpourings have begun to dry up. You feel a little drained, as if a thunderstorm has just passed. This is a time for taking it easy but not resting. It is a time for reflection and consideration. Did you take the right action? Were you too extreme in your reactions? Did you do all you could to push yourself forward and onward? The declining phase is after you have unleashed your true potential on the world and you take a step back to see the results.

You are still armed and ready but not taking any further action for the time being. You begin to stand down, begin the shutting-down process and start to put away your tools. It is a sort of physical tidy-up time. Your energy is beginning to ebb and you need to be looking forward to the next phase – resting.

The resting phase: This is exactly what it says – a time for resting. You need to recuperate, sleep, mend and nurture yourself. This isn't a time for physical activity or rushing about. You will seriously deplete your reserves if you take any action during the resting phase. You need to rest, put your feet up and do nothing.

The growing phase: After resting, the energy begins to move again. You wake refreshed and ready to face the next challenges. The spring has come and new sap is rising. You feel refreshed – or should do, if you have taken your rest seriously – and ready to push those new shoots up and out into the world. This might be a time for getting ready to go out into the world, both metaphorically and physically.

Fitting in with the phases

We know that we can't all adjust our lives to take into account the different phases because we live in the West and we are expected to do certain things in accord with everyone else and at the same time. But knowing about the phases means that we can treat ourselves more kindly. We know when we are at our best and what we can expect of ourselves. By taking it easy during a resting phase – even if we are at work, perhaps, and expected to be at our busiest – we might then be more productive during an agitated phase, if we have allowed ourselves to rest sufficiently.

The life cycle

Each of the three *dosha* has its own life cycle. Knowing when, during our lifetime, we might be more productive can save us a lot of frustration. If our career isn't taking off as quickly as we might like it to, it can be helpful to know that we may be a 'late starter' or that we might have already been through our agitated period and are now looking forward to some hard-earned rest.

	Childhood/ teens	Twenties/ thirties	Forties/ fifties	Sixties onwards
Vata	agitated	declining	resting	growing
Pitta	growing	agitated	declining	resting
Kapha	resting	growing	agitated	declining

The life cycle of the *vata dosha*: *Vata* are lively children indeed. They are full of life and often score considerable success while still extremely young. Child prodigies are all drawn

during their much later life and often seem suddenly to come to life again when most of us are thinking of retiring.

The life cycle of the *pitta dosha*: *Pitta* types are energetic and agitated in their twenties and thirties. They are the go-getters of industry. Young and sharp and very busy, they often take the business world by storm when others are still training and gaining experience. The latest trend of energetic entrepreneurs who are young and running dot.com companies are invariably drawn from the *pitta dosha*.

The life cycle of the *kapha dosha*: The *kapha dosha* is slower to get going. These people take their time building to a peak in their late middle age. As children they may seem sleepy (as indeed they are, since it is their resting phase) but don't write them off. They come good later in life and achieve success. They are the late starters. I know. I am *kapha dosha* and didn't write my first book until I was in my forties. But I do look forward to a very productive agitated phase which should see me through to my sixties.

Vaastu and the *dosha* of your home
The three *dosha* are three 'types' of people. But the principles apply to homes as well. Where you live has its own *dosha* and knowing what sort of home you have may be of some benefit when comparing it to your own *dosha*. For instance, you might be *kapha dosha* living in a *vata* house. Would this be suitable? Had you even considered that your home might have a 'personality' and that it might not suit your own?

We all have preferences about where we live and sometimes have to accommodate those preferences to fit in with partners and family. And sometimes we just live wherever we end up, without thinking about it. Vaastu is about making choices. If we consciously recognize that *where* we live might have repercussions on *how* we live, we can begin to make changes if necessary.

from the *vata dosha*. This doesn't mean they are finished once they have left childhood behind, but instead can capitalize on their earlier achievements. They enter a new phase of productivity

	Vata		*Pitta*		*Kapha*	
1. Age	new	❏	more than 20 years	❏	old	❏
2. Style	modern	❏	traditional	❏	period	❏
3. Construction	wood/metal	❏	brick	❏	stone	❏
4. Heating	electric	❏	gas/solid fuel	❏	wood/coal fire	❏
5. Roof	concrete tiles	❏	slate	❏	clay tiles	❏
6. Size	small/compact	❏	medium	❏	large/grand	❏
7. Floors	1	❏	2–3	❏	3+	❏
8. Fashion	contemporary	❏	comfortable	❏	substantial	❏
9. Furnishings	minimalist	❏	comfortable	❏	luxurious	❏
10. Location	city	❏	town	❏	countryside	❏
11. Occupants	1	❏	2–4	❏	4+	❏
12. Type	flat/apartment	❏	semi/terraced	❏	detached	❏

Above is a short questionnaire to help you find out what sort of home you have. If you tick the boxes you will invariably end up with a 'score' for one type of *dosha* – this is your home type.

You know your own *dosha*. Are the two compatible? If not, have you considered why not? Are you living in someone else's choice? Is their *dosha* compatible with the *dosha* of your/their home?

You should try to make sure that your own personal *dosha* and the *dosha* of your home are compatible if you want peace of mind. There is nothing more unsettling, according to Vaastu principles, than living 'wrong' – living in circumstances, location and a style that don't suit your individual make-up.

Work with what you've got

Remember, however, that there is no simple 'right' and 'wrong' about any of this. Being one sort of *dosha* is no better or worse than any other sort. There is no hierarchy or spiritual order. You are what you are and that is fine. You can't emulate another *dosha*,

nor aspire to be another sort. You get the hand you are dealt and have to play it as it lies. We make the best of what we've got and that's all there is to it. We might be able to adjust and change where and how we live but we can't turn a modern bungalow into a period country house – it just wouldn't work. Nor can we change our *dosha* for another sort just because we think we like the sound of another type. A lot of problems would be easily ironed out if people remembered that they have to work with what they've got. You often see the wrong additions to a house where the owner has tried to fake the age of their property or add a feature that is plainly unsuitable.

Interior design, which is a fundamental part of Vaastu, should also stick to this basic rule: work with what you've got. If you have a large sunny room there is no point in trying to make it dark and cosy. If you have a Victorian semi there is no point in trying to make it into a Georgian town house or a Tudor manor house. Likewise, having a grand country house and dividing it up into bedsits or small flats will only discourage good Vaastu and cause the house quickly to disintegrate.

Houses and the dosha cycle

Each and every house goes through the same cycles – growing, agitated, declining and resting. When your house is newly built and fresh it is in its growing stage. After a few years – depending on how long the house was built to last – it will enter its agitated stage, when it will excite and invigorate the occupants. Then it will enter its declining stage, when it begins to look a bit tatty and careworn. Finally, it will enter its resting stage, when it has ceased to decline

and is ramshackle and very old indeed; many ruins may be considered to be in their resting stage. If the house were then to be restored, it would begin the cycle over again and go back to its growing stage.

It should be fairly easy to work out which dosha stage your house is in. Ask yourself:

• Was it built recently? (growing)
• Does it inspire and excite? (agitated)
• Is it comfortable and 'mature'? (declining)
• Is it old and ramshackle? (resting)

We have taken a brief look here at the principles of *ayurveda*. We will return to the subject later in Chapter 7, when we consider the practical side. Now we need to have a look at the third of the three key aspects of Vaastu – *jyotish* astrology.

jyotish
astrology

Jyotish is a Sanskrit word derived from two root words – *jyoti*, which means 'light' and *isha*, which means 'lord'. *Jyotish* is therefore light of the Lord or Lord of light.

The light in this case is the light of the Sun, since the Sun is considered by Indian astrologers as being the soul of our universe – as indeed it was for a considerable time until it was realized that our solar system was merely a part of a greater whole.

The language of astrology

Jyotish uses precise mathematical calculations to establish exactly where all the major planets were at the very moment each person was born. You don't have to 'believe' in astrology for this information to work. Astrology uses a series of key words which describe just about every situation a human being can find themselves in. The words form a sort of universal language that we can all speak. This language, which gives everyone a unique snapshot of their birth, enables us to talk about problems, opportunities, obstacles and setbacks using the same sort of words. We all speak astrology

Western astrology grew out of Indian astrology, which is why there are so many similarities between them.

whether we believe in it or not. We all know what our sun sign is. We all know what that implies about us as a character or personality profile. We all have this information and all use it to a greater or lesser extent.

The use of astrology in India

Astrology is such an intrinsic part of Indian religious and cultural life that few people can go from day to day without some reference to it. It has many branches and types and is practised in virtually every home. *Jyotish* is fundamental to Hinduism and has been so since ancient times. References in the *Vedas* to certain eclipses have been used to date the texts to the fourth millennium BCE. One of the *vendangas* (auxiliary 'scientific' texts of the *Vedas*) is devoted to determining the right time for sacrifices.

At birth a horoscope is calculated and drawn up for every Hindu child by a professional astrologer. This gives auspicious and inauspicious dates for major events, such as when to start school, get married, undertake major business transactions and so on. There is even a *Jyotish* department at the Hindu University in Benares, which every year compiles the official Hindu astrological calendar – the *pancanga* – which sets out the exact dates for sacred days and the auspicious times for public events such as the state opening of parliament.

The naksatra

In *jyotish* much significance is given to the position of the Moon – the *naksatra*. The position of the Moon is known as its lunar mansion and is divided into 27 or 28 parts depending on the length of the month. The Moon occupies a different mansion or house every day and this position is used by astrologers to determine the prognosis of major diseases and ailments.

Hinduism

You may well ask what Hinduism is. And an answer is impossible. Hinduism is a religion, as well as a system of politics, a secular

lifestyle, a moral code, an ethical system and a set of social rules and laws. It has no central authority, no common creed, no senior law maker. Different Hindu sects follow different religious beliefs. Different Hindu gurus teach completely different practices. The breadth and scale of Hinduism are mind boggling. If anyone offers to explain Hinduism easily and simply they have either fooled themselves or are fooling you. Hinduism is the most fragmented and diverse religion/social system every to spring into being. There are only three basic issues that most, if not all, Hindus might agree on:

- a belief in the sacredness of the *Vedas* as revealed scriptures;
- *karma*;
- rebirth.

We looked at the *Vedas* earlier on, so perhaps a brief look here at the other two aspects of Hindu belief might be useful, since some knowledge of Hinduism will help us understand the thinking behind Vaastu.

Karma

The word *karma* comes from the *Upanishads* – the fourth and last part of the *Vedas* – and simply means 'action'. A human being is regarded as inextricably bound up in the cycle of birth and rebirth. Each of us accumulates merit based on our actions. We come into this life with *prarabdha karma*, which is what we have acquired in the previous life and what we have to work through. To determine our *prarabdha karma* we need to look at our *jyotish* astrology (more about this later). Once we know what we have brought with us, we can work towards paying back the karmic debt. This frees us from our prenatal *karma* and gives us liberation, assuming of course that we don't collect any more *karma* along the way, which of course we invariably do. Hindus attribute everything – good and bad fortune – to their *karma*. They also believe that any selfless acts do not accumulate *karma*. The cycle of birth and rebirth is known as *samsara* – the worldly cycle or wheel.

Rebirth (punarjanma)

We are born, we die. Most religions accept this. Hinduism believes that we return after each life, born again into a new life. Our role as humans is to break this *samsara*, this cycle, and attain a state of being reunited with *brahman*, God. Whether we can do this while still in a human form is debated. The nature of *brahman* is debated. The paths to achieving liberation are debated. All that Hindus agree on is that liberation is the goal and by working off our *karma* we can be freed from the cycle of birth and rebirth. The belief in how we get there and what happens to us when we do is dependent on which Hindu sect you subscribe to. The state of being reunited with *brahman* is not unlike the Buddhist state of *nirvana*. Buddhists also believe in the cycle of birth and rebirth and *karma*, a belief which comes directly from Hinduism.

Hinduism also believes in *enlightenment* – the moment when the whole knowledge of our existence suddenly becomes crystal clear. This idea of suddenly being bathed in light is very ancient indeed. This is where the 'light' part of the word *jyotish* comes in, since it was considered that the light of enlightenment was similar to the sudden burst of light from the Sun and that this light was to be found through *jnana* – knowledge of one's self.

The importance of time

Because Hindus believe in the cycle of birth and rebirth, the whole notion of time and repeating seasons and passages of time is very important. If we each have an allocated time, and a cycle within that time depending on our *dosha*, then time needs to be understood and categorized. There is a saying in the *Upanishads*:

Time cooks all things in the great self.
Those that know in what time is cooked are the knowers
of the Veda.

According to the Hindu belief system, time is divisible into various subdivisions. These are as follows:

* **1 *kalpa*** = 4,320,000 years
* **4 *yugas*** = 1 *kalpa*. We are living in the fourth *yuga* – *kali yuga*, the yuga of strife.
* **14 *manvantara*** = 1 *yuga*. Each *manvantara* is ruled over by a different patriarch, known as a *munu*.
* **1 day of Brahma** = one thousand years of the *Deva* – the gods. (Brahma is the creator of the universe and different from *brahman* in that Brahma has a personality and form – usually four-faced, with four arms holding a ladle, a string of pearls, a sceptre and a book of the *Veda* – whereas *brahman*, God, is formless.)
* **1 day and night of the *Deva*** = 1 human year
* **1 human year** = 6 seasons (*vasanta*, spring; *grisma*, heat; *varsa*, rain; *sarad*, autumn; *hemanta*, winter; *sisira*, coolness)
* **1 season** = 2 months – a dark lunar month, *krisnapaksa*, and a light lunar month, *suklapaksa*
* **1 lunar month** = 28 *naksatra*
* **1 *naksatra*** = 24 solar hours
* **24 solar hours** = 30 *muhurtas* (48 minutes each)
* **1 *muhurta*** = 2 *ghati* (24 minutes)
* **1 *ghati*** = 30 *kala* (48 seconds each)
* **1 *kala*** = 2 *pala* (24 seconds each)
* **1 *pala*** = 6 *prana* (4 seconds each)
* **1 *prana*** = 10 *vipala* (0.4 seconds each)
* **1 *vipala*** = 60 *prativipala* (0.000666 seconds each)

You may wonder, if this time division is so ancient, as indeed it is, how they measured such a minute amount of time as 0.000666 of a second. Your guess is as good as mine, but it certainly shows that there is a great deal about ancient India that we don't know and will probably never understand.

What this indicates is the incredible accuracy of Indian time-keeping and also how that accuracy was applied to astrological calculations. Astrologers were able to calculate exactly the moment a planet moved into a portion of the zodiac or became visible above the horizon. They understood astronomy in very precise detail. The marriage of astronomy and astrology has probably nowhere been closer than in India, where the two practices go side by side and have never been separated into science and 'magic', as they have in the West.

Jyotish and karma

In Indian astrology *karma* is subdivided into four distinct types.

Sanchita karma: This is a collection of all *karma*.

Prarabdha karma: This is the *karma* we bring with us from previous lives, and is also known as fate or destiny. It is the *karma* which has to be worked through in this life. It might not be all the *karma* we carry with us, but the relevant portion which it is considered we can cope with or are ripe for experiencing and eliminating.

Kriyamana karma: This is new *karma* that we are accumulating or generating in this life, the *karma* to be added to our total karmic resource to be taken forward into the next life.

Agama karma: This is our potential *karma* for the future. It is our intrinsic karmic nature and the way we view and deal with *karma*, the *karma* of our next life.

So, we have various types of *karma* to work with in Vaastu. *Sanchita karma* is said to be so deep and so unfathomable that no one can understand it, not even practitioners of *jyotish* and Vaastu. The other three could be described as past, present and future *karma*. Our past *karma* is also known as our *dridha karma* or fixed *karma*. Our present *karma* is known as our *dridha-adridha karma* or changeable *karma*. And our future *karma* is known as our *adridha karma* or, again, fixed *karma*. If we can only work with what we've got it makes sense to do something about the changeable *karma* – *dridha-adridha karma* or *kriyamana karma*. This is the *karma* we are accumulating and generating in this life.

We know that selfless acts produce no *karma* at all, but how do we free ourselves from the *karma* we are inadvertently building up in this life?

Indians consider all *karma* – both good and bad – to be something we seek to free ourselves from. Here in the West we tend to think of *karma* as a negative thing – only bad *karma*. If we wish to escape from the cycle of birth and rebirth we must free ourselves from all *karma*. When we have wiped the slate clean we can be reunited with *brahman* – not before. So we need to eliminate all *karma* and this is done by the practice of *upaya*. The *upaya* includes:

- chanting mantras – sacred syllables and prayers;
- fasting/feasting;
- worship of fire;
- understanding of the planets;
- devotion to the correct deities;
- specific acts of charity;
- wearing of holy gems, such as diamonds, rubies and emeralds.

However, just because you practise *upaya* doesn't mean that *karma* will automatically be eradicated. *Upaya* takes time – a lifetime in most cases – and results cannot be expected immediately. It is said that the shortest time in which *upaya* can work is 40 days, so don't expect miracles overnight.

For the purposes of Vaastu, the one *upaya* we are interested in is the understanding and knowledge of the planets – the *jyotish*

astrology. And we are only interested in a very small portion of it. Some people make a lifetime study of *jyotish* and still claim to know nothing of it as a subject. We don't need to go to such lengths. It is sufficient to grasp a few of the basics and take what we need for our understanding and practice of Vaastu.

The basics of *jyotish*

In Western astrology we are used to seeing our chart laid out in the form of a circle with the houses, planets and zodiac signs arranged around the edges. In Indian astrology they use a square, which is subdivided into the relevant houses, planets and zodiac signs. This square shape fits neatly and perfectly into the principles of Vaastu – as indeed it was designed to do.

In Western astrology we use 12 houses, the 12 zodiac signs and 10 planets (although, of course, two of these – the Sun and the Moon – aren't planets at all), the two nodes of the Moon and various aspects such as conjunctions, oppositions, trines, squares and sextiles. In *jyotish* everything is the same as in conventional Western astrology, except that it uses only seven planets (including the Sun and the Moon), and the two Moon nodes – Rahu and Ketu – are given much more prominence.

The seven planets of Indian astrology are:

- Sun
- Moon
- Mercury
- Mars
- Venus
- Jupiter
- Saturn

The missing ones are Uranus, Neptune and Pluto; the reason is that they simply weren't known about when *jyotish* was being developed all

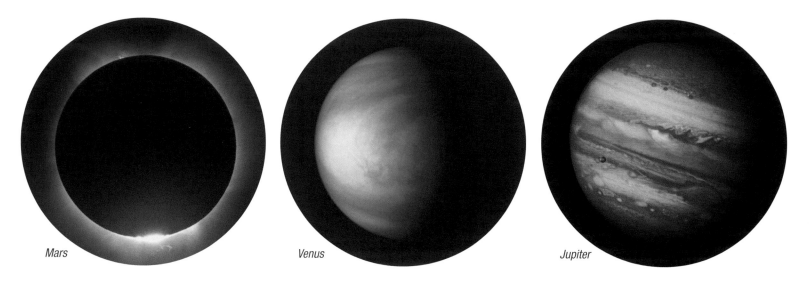

Mars *Venus* *Jupiter*

those thousands of years ago. Modern Indian astrologers are now working with them, but for the sake of Vaastu they can be discounted.

What the planets mean

Each of these seven planets is said to rule or govern certain aspects of life. It is interesting to look at these in relation to Vaastu.

Sun	Moon	Mercury	Mars	Venus	Jupiter	Saturn
organic matter and vegetation	organic matter and vegetation	living beings and vegetation	inorganic matter and minerals	organic matter and vegetation	living beings and vegetation	inorganic matter and minerals
pitta	*vata* and *kapha*	*vata*, *pitta* and *kapha*	*pitta*	*vata* and *kapha*	*kapha*	*vata*
four-legged creatures	rodents, reptiles, insects	flying creatures	four-legged creatures	two-legged creatures	two-legged creatures	flying creatures
bones	blood	skin	marrow and muscles	reproductive organs	fatty tissue	nerves
head	face	hips	chest	pelvis	abdomen	thighs
king	queen	prince/princess	army chief	advisor	chancellor	bodyguard
coarse/thick	new	cleanliness	variegated	strength	practical	age
dark red	white	green	bright red	blue	yellow	black
garnet	moonstone	peridot	bloodstone	white sapphire	citrine	lapis lazuli
the soul	the senses and the emotions	mental powers and speech	power and strength	desires and yearnings	knowledge and luck	lessons and obstacles
temples	watery places	sports arenas	fiery places	pleasure places	treasuries	dark places
east	north-west	north	south	south-east	north-east	west

Whilst this list is by no means exhaustive – it does in fact run to several thousand words in the *Vedas* – it gives an idea of how people in India view the importance of the planets and their relationship to us.

The zodiac signs

The 12 zodiac signs are the same in both Eastern and Western astrological systems. They use very similar symbolism and have the same sort of character analysis.

The *jyotish* symbols are:

- **Aries** – a ram
- **Taurus** – a bull
- **Gemini** – a man holding a club and a woman holding a stringed musical instrument
- **Cancer** – a crab
- **Leo** – a lion
- **Virgo** – a young woman in a boat holding wheat in one hand and fire in the other
- **Libra** – a man holding a set of scales
- **Scorpio** – a scorpion
- **Sagittarius** – a centaur holding a bow and arrow and about to fire the arrow
- **Capricorn** – a crocodile with the upper body of a deer or goat
- **Aquarius** – a man with a water container on his shoulder, about to pour
- **Pisces** – two fish swimming in opposite directions

These zodiac signs correspond to certain elements, as in the West.

- **Fire** – Aries, Leo, Sagittarius
- **Earth** – Taurus, Virgo, Capricorn
- **Air** – Gemini, Libra, Aquarius
- **Water** – Cancer, Scorpio, Pisces

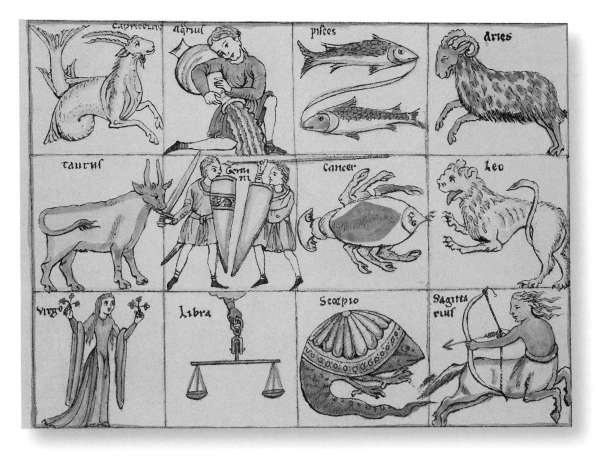

Zodiac sign	Compass direction	Part of the body ruled	Height	Place preferred
Aries	east	top of the head	short	woodlands
Taurus	south	face and throat	short	fields/meadows
Gemini	west	neck, shoulders, arms	average	villages
Cancer	north	chest	average	ponds/wells
Leo	east	abdomen above the navel	tall	mountains
Virgo	south	abdomen below the navel	tall	cultivated vegetation
Libra	west	pubic region	tall	busy market places
Scorpio	north	genitals	tall	caves
Sagittarius	east	thighs and hips	average	cities
Capricorn	south	knees	average	forests
Aquarius	west	calves	short	rural communities
Pisces	north	feet	short	lakes

You must remember, however, that we will be interested only in your rising or ascendant sign for the purposes of Vaastu, not your sun sign. More of this later.

The zodiac signs embody a lot of attributes that are missing in Western astrology but which are relevant to Vaastu. These include compass directions, *ayurveda* qualities, geographical locations, body size and type, and similar features. The chart above may help to explain all this. You can see that, for example, an Aries rising type of person might be short and prefer woodlands as a haunt. They would be likely to suffer from headaches and migraines (the part of the body ruled is also the part where problems are likely), use their head a lot and earn their living from mental activity. They are also likely to be happier in the east – this could mean either the culture of the East or facing that compass direction.

Your rising sign and your environment – the *parashara*

Your rising sign – and we will see shortly how to calculate this –

provides a lot of information with regard to Vaastu that maybe you had never been aware of or thought about. This is known as your *parashara* and in India it is accepted as part of your character and make-up – it is an intrinsic part of your nature. If you are feeling unhappy it might be that your *parashara* isn't being satisfied – you may be attempting to live in the wrong environment or in the wrong style. Once you know your rising sign it makes sense to learn and understand your *parashara*. The environment that corresponds to each zodiac sign is as follows:

- **Aries** – newly developed land, sandy soil, hilly places, unfrequented places, dangerous places, furnaces, ceilings, roofs, east walls of any buildings, places rich in natural resources especially gem stones and minerals.
- **Taurus** – grazing or agricultural land, anywhere farmers collect such as markets and inns, meadows, lawns, dim rooms with low ceilings, barns, basements, closets, storerooms, south-east walls of houses, anywhere below ground.
- **Gemini** – anywhere entertainers collect such as theatres, circuses, anywhere games are played, casinos, amusement arcades, anywhere within walking distance, interconnecting places, stairs, streets – especially at night, escalators, recreation rooms, west walls of houses, high levels.
- **Cancer** – fountains, pools, rivers, canals, plumbing, reservoirs, kitchens, laundry rooms, harbours, restaurants, north walls of buildings.
- **Leo** – rocky high places, steep places, inaccessible places, forts and castles, jungles, deserts, manor halls, disorderly places, east walls of houses.
- **Virgo** – artistic places, anywhere that artists frequent, places used by women, gardens, cornfields, granaries, pantries, rented rooms, libraries, medical places, south walls of any buildings.

- **Libra** – shops, merchants' houses, auction rooms, trade shows, public areas in houses, alcoves and wardrobes, west walls of buildings.
- **Scorpio** – anywhere venomous creatures live, swamps, hidden places, secret places, oil wells, sewers, underground pipe works, stagnant water, north-east walls of buildings.
- **Sagittarius** – temples, state residences, grand houses, majestic rooms, large rooms, ammunition rooms, stables, strong rooms and safes, south-east walls of buildings.
- **Capricorn** – uncultivated fields, run-down districts, barren fields, mines – especially disused ones, mountain peaks, cliffs, swampy woods, untidy and neglected rooms, dark rooms, pokey rooms, south walls of houses.
- **Aquarius** – unusual or unique places, communication rooms, scientific research establishments, antique shops, rooms furnished with antiques, antique medical equipment, antique communication equipment, north-west walls of buildings.
- **Pisces** – seas, beaches, damp places, prisons, monasteries, nunneries, hospitals, workhouses, therapy rooms, loud echoey places such as swimming pools, church halls, north-west walls of houses.

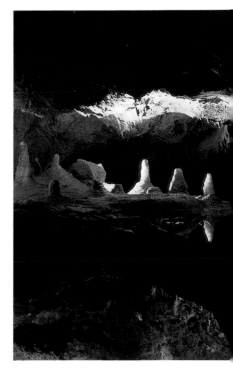

The houses

There are twelve houses in both conventional Western astrology and *jyotish*. Each of these houses covers an area of life experiences. If you know which zodiac sign your rising sign falls in and which house it occupies, you can discover a lot about your basic human nature. And this is vital in calculating where and how you should live for the purposes of Vaastu. These houses in *jyotish* are known as the twelve *bhava* – a state of mind or existence – and their meanings and interpretations were set down centuries ago and have remained largely unchanged.

First we need to see what a *jyotish* chart layout looks like so that we can see where the houses are.

You will notice that four of the houses occupy twice the space of the other eight. These four – the 1st, 4th, 7th and 10th – are considered to be the major houses and the others the minor houses. This doesn't mean that the others are less important, just that the major houses have all the really big stuff in them, like relationships, birth, health and career.

- 1st house – birth, character, appearance, behaviour, body, complexion, fame, dignity, happiness, constitution, longevity, nature, prestige, strength/weaknesses, virtue, youth.
- 2nd house – family, personal possessions, communication, savings, eating and drinking, speech, wealth, eyesight.
- 3rd house – brothers and sisters, hearing, writing, travel, the arts, parents' death, prowess, courage.
- 4th house – education, learning, study, land and property, happiness, houses, emotions, mother.

		2nd house				12th house		
3rd house				1st house				11th house
		4th house				10th house		
5th house				7th house				9th house
		6th house				8th house		

- 5th house – children, counsel, taste, discernment, style, intelligence, intuition, memory, books.
- 6th house – accidents, anxieties, debt, loss of property, diseases, enemies, digestion,cruelty, injuries, imprisonment, defeats.

- 7th house – love, relationships, pleasure, enjoyment, partners in business, moraL conduct, extra-marital affairs, sexual desires.

- 8th house – bankruptcy, excretion, sexual organs, inheritance, litigation, mystery, the occult, assassination, friendships, fears, secrets.

- 9th house – good luck, religion, father, charity, politics, vehicles, grandchildren, goals and dreams.

- 10th house – business, authority, commerce, career, projects, ambitions, science, trade, status, achievements, position, honour.

- 11th house – wealth, wishes, gifts, luxury, foreplay, education, gains, earned money.

- 12th house – endings, death, living abroad, hidden things, darkness, enemies, convalescence, confinements including imprisonment.

Key words for houses

For astrological purposes, each of these houses has several meanings, as you can see. In India an astrologer would examine your *jyotish* chart in some detail before making an interpretation. They would select which of the meanings attributed to the houses were applicable. But for Vaastu purposes we can narrow down these houses into one or two key words so you can see how it affects your house or any other building you are interested in.

- 1st house – you, your personality

- 2nd house – family, possessions

- 3rd house – communication, mental faculties

- 4th house – the home, education

- 5th house – children, pleasure

- 6th house – accidents, defeats

- 7th house – relationships, desires

- 8th house – sex, crime

- 9th house – travel, religious beliefs

- 10th house – ambitions, career

- 11th house – friends, inner goals

- 12th house – death, the unconscious

Just as a quick check, it might be worth having a look at your home and seeing where these areas fall within its layout.

The house layout in this diagram assumes you have your front door – the opening out into the world – in the east. This is regarded as the 'best' position. From here we communicate with the outside world – 3rd house – present our home – 4th house – and gather kudos from our children (remember that in India the more children you have, the greater your prestige, prowess and reputation) – 5th house.

Conversely, we have hiding at the 'back' of the house our religious beliefs – 9th house – as they are a private matter, and our

unconscious – 12th house – as, again, it is a private thing. Sex – 8th house – is also hidden away here and so are our friends – 11th house – or rather they are allowed into the deepest heart of our home since we trust and respect them with our privacy.

Now what happens if your front door isn't facing due east? Well, we will go into this in more detail in the practical section, but it throws a new light on what you are presenting to the world – and we need to know what zodiac signs are in each house since this affects the way in which you present your life to the outside world. But suppose your house faced due south. Then it would be your relationships that were of prime importance to you and that is what you would be 'advertising' about yourself. If you faced due west it might be your ambitions that were on display. And if due north

then your outer personality – 1st house – would be what you were showing the world, since this is the house of charisma and ego.

We will cover all this in later chapters in some depth. This is just a quick look to whet your appetite and get you thinking about how the world sees you – and, more important, how you present yourself to the world and what you show in private.

The zodiac *lagna*

The position of the houses is known as the *bhava* and the position of the zodiac signs is known as the *lagna*. You need to know both the *lagna* and the *bhava* to construct a Vaastu *jyotish* chart. The *lagna* has the same design as the *bhava*, with Aries occupying the 1st house position.

However, whichever zodiac sign is the rising sign occupies that top position, so your rising sign always occupies the first house. The first house is you, if you like, and the other houses represent what happens to you and around you.

Suppose your rising sign was Leo. Then Leo would occupy the first house position, in place of Aries.

From this you can see that the zodiac signs are rotated, but the houses are not. Suppose Scorpio was your rising sign. You can now see which other signs occupy which houses, as shown in the diagram opposite. Once we know the key words for each sign we can get an idea of how those house characteristics will manifest in our life and environment.

The zodiac meanings

Once we have worked out the house positions in relation to our home – this is *what* we show to the world – then we can work out the zodiac signs, which represent the *manner* in which we

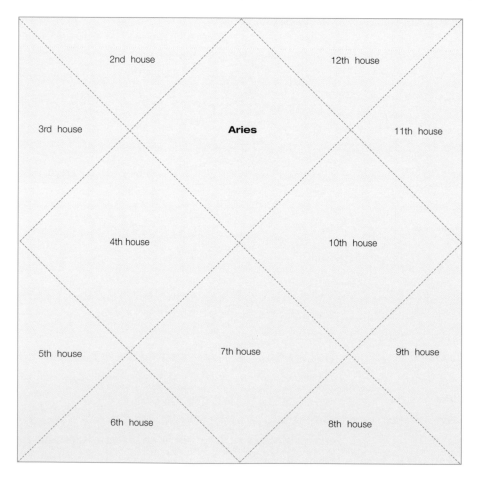

2nd house **Sagittarius**		12th house **Libra**
3rd house **Capricorn**	1st house **Scorpio**	11th house **Virgo**
4th house **Aquarius**		10th house **Leo**
5th house **Pisces**	7th house **Taurus**	9th house **Cancer**
6th house **Aries**		8th house **Gemini**

The Scorpio bhava and lagna

present ourselves. Certain characteristics are attached to each zodiac sign.

- **Aries** is a masculine sign. It is the first sign of the zodiac. Aries is a cardinal fire sign. Keywords for Aries are *urgent* and *assertive*.

- **Taurus** is a feminine sign. It is the second sign of the zodiac. Taurus is a fixed earth sign. Keywords for Taurus are *determined* and *honourable*.

- **Gemini** is a masculine sign. It is the third sign of the zodiac. Gemini is a mutable air sign. Keywords for Gemini are *versatile* and *expressive*.

- **Cancer** is a feminine sign. It is the fourth sign of the zodiac. Cancer is a cardinal water sign. Keywords for Cancer are *intuitive and emotional*.

- **Leo** is a masculine sign. It is the fifth sign of the zodiac. Leo is a fixed fire sign. Keywords are *powerful* and *dramatic*.

- **Virgo** is a feminine sign. It is the sixth sign of the zodiac. Virgo is a mutable earth sign. Keywords for Virgo are *discriminating* and *analytical*.

- **Libra** is a masculine sign. It is the seventh sign of the zodiac. Libra is a cardinal air sign. Keywords for Libra are *harmony* and *diplomacy*.

- **Scorpio** is a feminine sign. It is the eighth sign of the zodiac. Scorpio is a fixed water sign. Keywords for Scorpio are *passion* and *power*.

- **Sagittarius** is a masculine sign. It is the ninth sign of the zodiac. Sagittarius is a mutable fire sign. Keywords for Sagittarius are *freedom* and *optimism*.

- **Capricorn** is a feminine sign. It is the tenth sign of the zodiac. Capricorn is a cardinal earth sign. Keywords for Capricorn are *duty* and *discipline*.

- **Aquarius** is a masculine sign. It is the eleventh sign of the zodiac. Aquarius is a fixed air sign. Keywords for Aquarius are *independence* and *compassion*.

- **Pisces** is a feminine sign. It is the last and twelfth sign of the zodiac. Pisces is a mutable water sign. Keywords for Pisces are *nebulous* and *receptive*.

The qualities of the elements

From the list of zodiac signs you will notice that each sign is given a descriptive word – fixed, mutable, cardinal – before its element. These describe the manner in which the sign likes to express itself. The fixed signs like things to stay the way they are; the mutable signs are versatile and adaptable to change; the cardinal signs like to instigate change. The way these signs approach change is expressed through their elements. For instance, both Aries and Cancer are cardinal signs – they like to spark off new projects, they don't stand still, they are natural leaders and full of ideas. But Aries is a fire sign, which means it will express this influence in a very outgoing, enthusiastic way, whereas Cancer will express it through water, which is much more emotional and intuitive.

The importance of astrology in India

In the West most of us know what our own sun sign (the zodiac sign) means. If we were born a Sagittarius, for instance, we might know that represents us as liking travel and being open-minded and philosophical. We might even know our partner's sun sign. But usually, unless we study the subject of astrology in any depth, that's about it. In India everyone knows about astrology because it permeates every level of Indian life in a very real and significant way.

You can't practise Vaastu unless you know what the houses mean, what the sun signs mean, how to interpret a basic chart, how to align the houses, how to calculate your ascendant. In the West astrology has become merely a light-hearted sort of listing in the daily newspapers. But in India it is still very much a living and serious subject. No one in India would dream for a moment of getting married without both parties consulting an astrologer. And a lot of marriages in India are still 'arranged'. Who do you think does much of the arranging? Of course, the astrologer. And the system in a way works because compatibility is worked out very carefully in advance before the marriage. A system as complex and as longlasting as this doesn't endure unless it works. The success of the arranged marriage system (and it doesn't matter what anyone's personal views about it are at this stage) is exactly that – a success laid down over countless generations and centuries. It works because there is something very real and fundamental going on behind the scenes before the arrangement takes place – the synastry. The synastry is the matching of two horoscopes or charts to see if they are compatible.

In Vaastu we do a similar thing – match you with your home. If there is no compatibility, then of course you will suffer problems. If you and your home are compatible, you will find happiness and contentment.

Understanding the houses and zodiac signs

Don't forget, again, we will be dealing in Vaastu with your rising or ascending sign for the *jyotish*, not your sun sign. How to calculate this is coming next, but first let's have a quick look at how these zodiac signs affect the manner in which we express ourselves to the world.

Suppose you have your 4th house in Aries. The 4th house is all about the home. Aries is expressed urgently and assertively. What might that tell you about this person? That they place great emphasis on their home, regard it as of great importance and need to create a 'perfect' place to live with grandeur and style, perhaps? That's about the interpretation a Vaastu consultant would place on it. And if they were living in a bedsit you could see that their home and their *jyotish* would be out of line – incompatible, if you like. Changes would have to be made to bring the basic generic personality more in harmony with their *jyotish*.

Calculating your ascendant or rising sign

The constellation that was appearing over the horizon when you were born is of great importance in both Vaastu and *jyotish*. Your sun sign – the one you read in horoscopes – is the constellation the Sun was in when you were born. Knowing your ascendant isn't as easy as knowing your sun sign. We all know our sun sign from the date we were born, but calculating your rising sign is a little more complex but not too difficult. You need to know your zodiac sign from your date of birth, and you need to know your time of birth.

Use the chart below to look up your birth sign along the top and your time of birth down the left-hand side. Where the two meet is your rising or ascendant sign. This chart seems to work extremely well for most ascendants. Obviously you need to make sure you have remembered to add on an hour for British Summer Time if you were born during the summer months.

The characteristics of the ascendant signs

If you are unfamiliar with how the ascendant expresses itself, here is a brief outline of each of the twelve ascendants.

Aries ascendant

Since Aries rules the head, it is only natural that those with Aries ascending have a strong desire to 'head butt' whatever arises in life. An Aries ascendant gives you drive, ambition, aggressiveness and often a bit of impulsiveness. Aries ascending should guard against lack of follow-through. They are individualistic and impatient, and may have too many irons in the fire at the same time. The fire sign makes them rather quick-tempered. They may be inclined to blush easily or turn red in the face when angered, but they tend to cool

	Aries	Taurus	Gemini	Cancer	Leo	Virgo	Libra	Scorpio	Sagittarius	Capricorn	Aquarius	Pisces
6–8 am	Taurus	Gemini	Cancer	Leo	Virgo	Libra	Scorpio	Sagittarius	Capricorn	Aquarius	Pisces	Aries
8–10 am	Gemini	Cancer	Leo	Virgo	Libra	Scorpio	Sagittarius	Capricorn	Aquarius	Pisces	Aries	Taurus
10 am–noon	Cancer	Leo	Virgo	Libra	Scorpio	Sagittarius	Capricorn	Aquarius	Pisces	Aries	Taurus	Gemini
noon–2 pm	Leo	Virgo	Libra	Scorpio	Sagittarius	Capricorn	Aquarius	Pisces	Aries	Taurus	Gemini	Cancer
2–4 pm	Virgo	Libra	Scorpio	Sagittarius	Capricorn	Aquarius	Pisces	Aries	Taurus	Gemini	Cancer	Leo
4–6 pm	Libra	Scorpio	Sagittarius	Capricorn	Aquarius	Pisces	Aries	Taurus	Gemini	Cancer	Leo	Virgo
6–8 pm	Scorpio	Sagittarius	Capricorn	Aquarius	Pisces	Aries	Taurus	Gemini	Cancer	Leo	Virgo	Libra
8–10 pm	Sagittarius	Capricorn	Aquarius	Pisces	Aries	Taurus	Gemini	Cancer	Leo	Virgo	Libra	Scorpio
10 pm–midnight	Capricorn	Aquarius	Pisces	Aries	Taurus	Gemini	Cancer	Leo	Virgo	Libra	Scorpio	Sagittarius
midnight–2 am	Aquarius	Pisces	Aries	Taurus	Gemini	Cancer	Leo	Virgo	Libra	Scorpio	Sagittarius	Capricorn
2–4 am	Pisces	Aries	Taurus	Gemini	Cancer	Leo	Virgo	Libra	Scorpio	Sagittarius	Capricorn	Aquarius
4–6 am	Aries	Taurus	Gemini	Cancer	Leo	Virgo	Libra	Scorpio	Sagittarius	Capricorn	Aquarius	Pisces

quickly. They champion independence and freedom, and are outspoken in most of their opinions. They are capable of quick action and getting things done fast. Red may be a favourite colour.

Aries ascending tends to better-than-average height, spare body, rather elongated face and neck. The complexion is often ruddy; the hair may be red or 'sandy'. The frontal area of the head is usually pronounced. The eyebrows may be heavy and tend to bridge the nose. The forehead can be rather wide and the chin pointed. There may be scars or marks about the head. In the male, the Adam's apple may protrude more than normal.

Taurus ascendant

Taurus rules the throat. Therefore, it is to be expected that Taurus ascending

places emphasis on this area of the individual. There may be some talent, or at least more than a passing interest, in singing and public speaking. The throat also has much to do with the appetites: all Taureans love food and drink and with a Taurus ascendant there is no exception to this. An emphasis on satisfying the 'appetites' of the body is likely.

These people are endowed with great self-reliance, are easy-going, but possess a strongly persistent and determined nature. Taurus ascending is highly attuned to practical and material matters – money and their possessions. They are basically kind and loving but inclined to frequent stubbornness, and jealousy. They greatly enjoy the seeking of pleasure. Tempers are not

easily aroused, but they can be violent if pushed too far. They are usually patient and willing to wait for success.

Taurus ascending usually gives a solid, hard body of about average height. There is a tendency to plumpness of the torso. Usually, the face is square, the neck rather short and big. There is a general fullness to all the facial and bodily features. The eyes may be prominent or slightly protruding. The hair tends to the lighter shades of brown. The shoulders may be wide and square, and the chest thick. The nostrils may be flared, especially when the person is angry. The hands may be somewhat podgy.

Gemini ascendant

Gemini ascending tends to make the person quick and quick-witted. Gemini controls the hands, arms and nervous system generally, so the individual is likely to be interested in using the hands, as well as the mind. This ascendant gives a probing, curious mind which is constantly on the alert for anything new or different. There is a desire to acquire knowledge and to experiment. The person feels a great need to communicate with others, both verbally and with the written word. Gemini ascendant gives the person a dual nature and they may have income from more than one source or pursue two careers at the same time. Gemini ascending should guard against being just a 'jack-of-all-trades' and develop more persistence. Normally, Gemini ascending causes the person to be rather slender, erect and of average or less-than-average height. The legs frequently are thin and a bit bird-like. They seldom have an excessive weight problem because of their abundant nervous energy. The body is best described as wiry. The arms tend to be rather long and thin; fingers may be the same. The face seems to be 'double' – there may be a cleft in the chin and even the nose, which may be slightly hooked and sometimes reddish. Hair tends to be dark brown.

Cancer ascendant

Cancer, whose ruler is the Moon, relates to the stomach – the holder and collector of that which sustains life (a point and source of pleasure and comfort). Emotions and inner feelings play a major role in this ascendant's mode of living. There is an acute sensitivity to all persons and conditions nearby. Usually, there is a fertile imagination, sentimentality, as well as a sympathetic and talkative nature. Typically there is a great fondness for the home, mother, and sometimes the father. Cancer ascending tends to give a strongly emotional nature and extreme sensitivity to any criticism. They love the past, the fireside, their comforts, food, the kitchen, and just about everything that is traditional. With this ascendant, the individual will make a practice of 'collecting' either material things, personalities, and/or experiences.

Cancer ascendants are often nicely curved. Adults frequently have rather broad hips and tend to put on a bit of weight in that area. Height is normally short to medium. The arms may have a crab-like motion; legs tend to be short and stocky. Feet and hands may be small and delicate. There may be a noticeable undulating gait to the walk. The face is usually round-moon-shaped, and the profile may be inwardly curved as the Moon appears when not full.

Leo ascendant

Leo ascending usually makes for a bright and sunny disposition and a strong character. Often there is a magnetic personal appeal that begets admiration, just what Leo wants most. The person is normally good-natured and generous – sometimes overly so. They are inclined to speak frankly, loudly and with a flair that stimulates listeners to buy or believe. This ascendant is demonstrative and possessed of great energy. There is a strong desire and need to be the centre of attention, to 'show off'. The Leo ascendant is basically good-humoured, popular and of a rather regal disposition. There may be a tendency and desire to 'run' the lives of friends. Generally, these individuals are the 'hand shakers' and 'back slappers' of the zodiac.

Leo ascending is normally tall, broad-shouldered and large of frame. There is a tendency to put on weight after a streamlined youth. Often the hair appears 'sunshine bright'. The smile may be broad and beaming. The brisk walk and carriage is regal – full of pride and dignity, and may be even pompous at times. On many, the hair grows low and thick on the neck, much as the lion's mane. Everything about the face seems to be generous in size and proportion.

Virgo ascendant

Virgo ascending is constantly assimilating, evaluating and criticizing. There is generally a liking for work but too much worry over any lack of perfection in the work that is done. This rising sign tends to endow those with Virgo ascendant with a self-critical attitude, which leads to modesty and often a feeling of inferiority. The individual is basically conservative, diplomatic, tactful and somewhat highly strung. There may be a good amount of shrewdness and a strong desire for money. Virgo ascending learns readily and quickly and has a deep desire to tell others how to improve themselves. They are often too inclined to 'tell it like it is'.

Virgo ascending tends to average height, average weight, and an angular but solid build. Usually, the shoulders and hips are fairly wide. It may be easy to tack on a few pounds of extra weight. Facial features are typically small but nicely shaped. The nose may be slightly hooked at the end. Complexion tends to be fair and smooth. The bone structure of the face usually makes this type quite photogenic. The walk is often smooth and graceful. Generally, the appearance might be described as 'clean-cut'.

Libra ascendant

Libra rules the kidneys and lower back. The kidneys, through their elimination of wastes and poisons from the body, tend to maintain balance and harmony. Libra ascending is concerned with 'maintaining balance' in the affairs of mankind and is a believer in justice for all. This ascendant typically is a lover of beauty and order, and seeks to bring harmony and balance into their lives and the lives of friends. There is a tendency to matchmaking, party-giving and partying in general. Libra ascending prefers the good life, surrounded by all that is beautiful in colour, symmetry and taste. This ascendant makes for a courteous, pleasant and agreeable person. Sometimes there is a tendency to meddle too much in others' affairs. This person may be the champion of the underdog.

Usually, the body is well formed, inclined to be tall, slender, with a tendency toward stoutness in middle age. The hair is well kept and typically dark or black in colour. Because of the Venus influence, many Libra ascendants can be termed 'beautiful' in appearance. Features usually are nicely shaped; teeth may be 'pearly', lips generous and finely chiselled. Many have naturally curly hair. Usually, there is a pleasant roundness to all features.

Scorpio ascendant

Scorpio rules the secret places – the organs of reproduction and elimination. This rulership gives the Scorpio ascendant an intense drive and desire to produce results – and to do away with whatever stands in the way of this desire. It is a good ascendant for ultimate success because of the strength, intensity, drive, determination and aggressiveness it tends to give the person. The ambition to succeed is powerful – sometimes too strong for the individual's own good. Scorpio ascending is tenacious, determined, secretive, penetrating, critical, suspicious, emotional and often blunt in speech and actions. The Scorpio ascendant is alert, forceful, and seemingly fond of contest. Purposes and goals are realized if not by subtlety, then by strength of will – or force if necessary. Luxury is appreciated, but they can be very frugal if that is what is required to achieve success.

The height of Scorpio ascending is usually above average. The body tends to be stout and the face may seem 'stuffed' or 'puffy'. The eyes may be large and penetrating; they may be the outstanding facial feature. Hair typically is black, thick, coarse, often curly. The nose may be seen as 'Roman'. Skin might be sallow and somewhat oily. The walk may be quick and 'bouncy'.

Sagittarius ascendant

Sagittarius rules the thighs and hips, which are the prime movers in enabling someone to travel far, to stand, to sit and to enjoy a full measure of life. This ascendant causes the person to be jolly, good natured and hearty, a witty and adept conversationalist – capable of telling a good story now and then. These people have a

white in later years. There is often a tendency to stamp or scrape the feet.

Capricorn ascendant

Capricorn rules the knees, which enable us to raise ourselves to our maximum height but which are also subject to bending quickly and are quite vulnerable to blows and injury. Capricorn ascending inclines the individual to a serious personality – heavy and grave. There is much practicality, caution, and prudence in all actions. This ascendant is status- and success-oriented and never fails to use whatever is near as the attempt to climb higher is made. Capricorn ascending is basically an opportunist, constantly striving, frequently failing, but always persisting in the climb to higher levels of achievement. The person may seem cold, even snobbish at times. Sometimes a sense of humour may be so well concealed that very few ever see it in action. This ascendant is highly practical.

somewhat uncanny ability to meet and become 'old friends' with total strangers quickly, mainly because of their ability to make others feel important. This ascendant likes to travel and likes the great outdoors in both a physical and mental sense. There is a strong desire for freedom of thought and action. They tend to be frank and honest to the letter. They may be inclined to be somewhat impatient and impulsive, which may cause frequent changes of interests. They generally like things done on a grand scale.

'Distinguished looking' is a term which will describe many with Sagittarius ascending. The person may be rather tall and large but not overweight until well past middle age. The face tends to be roundish and jovial, somewhat elongated. The teeth may be large and can protrude. The hair is dark in youth but impressively

The stature is normally average to slightly less than average. The chest area is usually rather flat and the body in general tends towards being lean, except for the legs, which more likely than not will be heavy. Ankles frequently are thick. The facial features may tend to be rather small and sharp or pointed in appearance. Often the skin and hair will be darker than other members of the same family not having Capricorn ascending. The hair is very dark, often black.

Aquarius ascendant

Aquarius rules the calves and ankles, which are subject to many changes as we move forwards and walk. Basically,

		Aries	Taurus	Gemini
ASCENDANT	**Aries**	urgent	determined urgent	versatile urgent
	Taurus	urgent determined	determined	versatile determined
	Gemini	urgent versatile	determined versatile	versatile
	Cancer	urgent intuitive	determined intuitive	versatile intuitive
	Leo	urgent powerful	determined powerful	versatile powerful
	Virgo	urgent analytical	determined analytical	versatile analytical
	Libra	urgent harmonious	determined harmonious	versatile harmonious
	Scorpio	urgent passionate	determined passionate	versatile passionate
	Sagittarius	urgent freedom	determined freedom	versatile freedom
	Capricorn	urgent duty	determined duty	versatile duty
	Aquarius	urgent independent	determined independent	versatile independent
	Pisces	urgent receptive	determined receptive	versatile receptive

the Aquarius-ascending person is kind, sociable, original, tolerant, generally broadminded about most things, and intellectual. There is much curiosity about and a delving into the occult and the 'off-beat' areas of life. This ascendant may cause the person to be regarded as eccentric in some ways. Aquarius rising wants attention and admiration from a wide circle of friends. The individual may smile a lot, even when not happy. The general manner is abrupt. There is usually more than a passing interest in wide-scale reform for the benefit of all humankind.

Aquarius ascending often gives what might be termed a 'striking' appearance. Height tends to be average to above. The build is full or square in most respects. The waist may be long. The facial features are usually rather even and might be called 'handsome'. This ascendant probably has an excellent profile. The walk may be sudden and eccentric – like the thinking processes of this unpredictable person.

Pisces ascendant

Pisces rules the feet. Just as the feet are sometimes uncertain about which is the next step or which way to turn next, so is Pisces ascending. This ascendant gives the individual a high-voltage nature and a dreamy, imaginative, sensitive and intellectually creative personality. Pisces ascending tends to get along well with all types of people until let down or disappointed in one way or another.

					SUN SIGN			
Cancer	Leo	Virgo	Libra	Scorpio	Sagittarius	Capricorn	Aquarius	Pisces
intuitive urgent	powerful urgent	analytical urgent	harmonious urgent	passionate urgent	freedom urgent	duty urgent	independent urgent	receptive urgent
intuitive determined	powerful determined	analytical determined	harmonious determined	passionate determined	freedom determined	duty determined	independent determined	receptive determined
intuitive versatile	powerful versatile	analytical versatile	harmonious versatile	passionate versatile	freedom versatile	duty versatile	independent versatile	receptive versatile
intuitive	powerful intuitive	analytical intuitive	harmonious intuitive	passionate intuitive	freedom intuitive	duty intuitive	independence intuitive	receptive intuitive
intuitive powerful	powerful	analytical powerful	harmonious powerful	passionate powerful	freedom powerful	duty powerful	independent powerful	receptive powerful
intuitive analytical	powerful analytical	analytical	harmonious analytical	passionate analytical	freedom analytical	duty analytical	independent analytical	receptive analytical
intuitive harmonious	powerful harmonious	analytical harmonious	harmonious	passionate harmonious	freedom harmonious	duty harmonious	independent harmonious	receptive harmonious
intuitive passionate	powerful passionate	analytical passionate	harmonious passionate	passionate	freedom passionate	duty passionate	independent passionate	receptive passionate
intuitive freedom	powerful freedom	analytical freedom	harmonious freedom	passionate freedom	freedom	duty freedom	independent freedom	receptive freedom
intuitive duty	powerful duty	analytical duty	harmonious duty	passionate duty	freedom duty	duty	independent duty	receptive duty
intuitive independent	powerful independent	analytical independent	harmonious independent	passionate independent	freedom independent	duty independent	independent	receptive independent
intuitive receptive	powerful receptive	analytical receptive	harmonious receptive	passionate receptive	freedom receptive	duty receptive	independent receptive	receptive

Secrets are enjoyed. There is generally subtlety and non-aggressiveness in the approach made to others, and to life in general. There may be a strong tendency toward indecisiveness, and they are hard to pin down when faced with the need to decide or to act. Pisces ascending is idealistic, impressionable, apt in detail, and orderly in manner. Feelings run very deep.

Pisces ascending tends to be relatively small and well proportioned. They may put on extra weight later in life. Arms and legs are usually short; hands may be small and 'artistic'. This ascendant tends often to give the individual large, dreamy eyes and long, thick lashes. The mouth and lips may be soft and sensitive, the nose small and well formed. There is a tendency towards a double chin, even a triple chin if much overweight. The feet may be unusual in some way.

These attributes obviously apply to your ascendant sign. But each sun sign will transform the ascendant. For instance, an Aries with a Scorpio ascendant will be quite different from an Aries with a Cancer ascendant. You need to match the key words for each sign to get a better overview. Suppose you were Leo sun sign and Scorpio ascendant. The Leo key word is *powerful* and the Scorpio ascendant key word is *passionate* – put them together and you get a very powerfully passionate person indeed. Suppose your sun sign was Pisces and your ascendant Taurus. Put those two together and you get *receptive* and *determined*: what would you make of this? How about a Libra sun sign – *harmonious* – and a Gemini ascendant – *versatile*? How would you describe that person?

Ascendants, houses and rooms

Now we've covered the ascendant signs and the houses as far as the person is concerned, the concept can be transferred easily to your home. Each house represents an area of the ground-plan of your home – or even an individual room. Your ascendant goes in the north and you overlay the zodiac signs on the houses to give you an interpretation for your home and its rooms.

Whose ascendant?

In traditional Indian culture the ascendant used would have been that of the 'head' of the household. This would usually have been the man. Nowadays it would be considered unacceptable for anyone to dominate a household by the mere fact of being the 'breadwinner' or being 'male'. So we should do this exercise for everyone in the house and see how compatible everyone is.

Zodiac ascendant signs

Aries – invigorating

Taurus – solid

Gemini – dual purpose

Cancer – comfortable

Leo – stimulating

Virgo – orderly

Libra – harmonious

Scorpio – passionate

Sagittarius – uninhibited

Capricorn – practical

Aquarius – unconventional

Pisces – nurturing

Key words for Vaastu

The key words we used previously referred to human personality types. For Vaastu the key words need to be changed to fit in with house styles, decor and furnishings. Listed below are the key words for both the ascendant signs and the houses for the Vaastu of your home.

Houses

1st house – personal room: Study, office, workshop, hobby room, administrative centre, headquarters.

2nd house – family room: Playroom, sitting room, anywhere the family congregates; also possessions room, which could be art collection or store rooms.

3rd house – communication room: Telephones, computers, windows to the outside world, the place where you write letters; but also room of transport – could be garage, car port, hallway for storing bicycle.

4th house – entrance: Ideally the place for the main door, or anywhere that leads to the outside world.

5th house – children's room, pleasure rooms: Could be dining room or ballroom for parties.

6th house – work room: Could be a sewing room, workshop, or office if you work from home.

7th house – relationship room: Could be bedroom, private sitting room, kitchen – wherever partners get together to be close and loving.

8th house – room of passion: This could for sex, fiery arguments, debating, or indulging whatever is your passion.

9th house – inner sanctum: This could be the ideal place for your pooja room or mediation retreat – it could be a bedroom if you feel safe and relaxed there.

10th house – relaxation room: Here you can read and dream, plan and study, chill out and just be you.

11th house – social room: Here you can entertain friends, socialize and relax in comfort.

12th house – exit: Back door, exit to garage or garden; it could be a utility room or a bin store; or it could be the bedroom, where you exit the day and enter the night.

The Aries ascendant house

Let's work through an example to see where the rooms fall and how the key words affect each area. This is for an Aries ascendant.

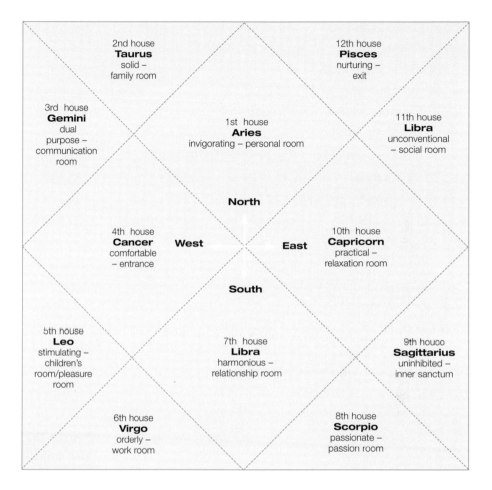

In an ideal world this person would have their front door along the west wall, to open into their 4th house area. Here they would present a comfortable aspect to the world – and what could be better than offering comfort to their visitors? Let's look at each of these areas in turn to give you an idea of what we can glean about this person from this example.

1st house – Aries (invigorating/personal room): They can use this room for whatever they want and here they will feel charged and enthusiastic. If this is their study or office they will work well, enjoy their time here, produce sharp work and generally feel invigorated and energetic. This is a good place for getting on with work rather than making another coffee and putting your feet up.

2nd house – Taurus (solid/family room): This room provides the nucleus for the family, somewhere they can gather and be together. Having this in the second house – the one of stability and strength – is a good thing. A family needs to be robust to survive. A family needs a strong place to feel free enough to relax in and be part of a team.

3rd house – Gemini (dual purpose/communication room): This is a good place to have a communication room as it doesn't have to be entirely dedicated to this one purpose. It might be an entrance hall with a telephone, but it can also be used to store coats and wellies, hang pictures, and be a welcoming room to receive visitors.

4th house – Cancer (comfortable/entrance): A front door along the west wall is a good place as it catches the evening sun. A comfortable entrance tells the world that the person is comfortable in their place in the world.

5th house – Leo (stimulating/children's room/pleasure rooms): It is a good idea for a children's room to be stimulating. By stimulating children you help them to become creative and productive members of society. In India a pleasure room is exactly that – for pleasure. Here people can lounge around and be decadent, and do it in a stimulating and creative way. This room can be furnished with luxurious fabrics and over-the-top style and taste. Children love bright colours – just look at the range of modern toys, all in bright primary colours to attract them – and you cannot overdo it in this area.

6th house – Virgo (orderly/work room): If someone needs to have a work room then it makes sense to locate it in the south area of the 6th house, where orderliness and tidiness may well contribute to the efficiency of the room. An untidy, cluttered room will cause discomfort and chaotic thinking.

7th house – Libra (harmonious/relationships): Harmony is what we need to create a good working and loving relationship that will endure and survive setbacks and problems. Here the person can relax with their partner and make plans for the future in a calm and balanced state.

8th house – Scorpio (passionate/passion room): A good place indeed for passion – the south-east corner is one of fast-moving energy, enthusiasm, creativity and experimentation. Here lovers can delight in each other's sexuality.

9th house – Sagittarius (uninhibited/inner sanctum): When someone wants to meditate they need to feel free, relaxed, protected and uninhibited. This is a good place to do it. The east here, as in the room for passion, allows them to let their hair down but in a different way. Here they can reveal their true self to nothing but the infinity of the cosmos itself. They need to feel totally at ease and unrestricted in any way.

10th house – Capricorn (practical/relaxation room): Relaxing is a skill we all need to learn. We need to do it in a focused way. Relaxing is important and being practical about it is no bad thing. Here someone could set up an exercise bike, a couch, a hammock – whatever it is they feel they need to chill out. This is a room, or an area, where you go specifically to relax and not just watch TV or sit down at the end of a long day.

11th house – Aquarius (unconventional/social room): With their friends a person can be themselves, let their hair down. For the serious visitor they might need a more formal room, decorated traditionally and tastefully. But for their friends who know the real

person they can be less cautious and decorate in a style that allows them to be wild and wacky – unconventional indeed.

12th house – Pisces (nurturing/exit): This is the place for the back door, a place to store the wellies for the kids to use as they run in and out of the garden. This is a place to build a veranda to catch the morning sun and allow the inhabitants to wake up before taking on the world anew each day.

Looking at rooms

We have seen how these zodiac signs and houses affect the overall shape of the house, but how does Vaastu work with the actual rooms in a house? Here is a ground-plan of a house with the same Aries ascendant, so you can see how it fits together.

Sitting room

This incorporates the family room, which is excellent, and part of the personal room, which is good, but some of the personal room lies in a corridor and in the laundry room. A better use of space could be made here by, perhaps, taking down the internal walls and moving them to create a self-contained personal room in the northern sector. The sitting room also incorporates the comfortable Cancer entrance, which is good, as the door into the sitting room lies right in the middle of this important area. The dual-purpose Gemini communication area is also in the sitting room, which might well be

where the TV and/or telephone should be positioned.

Dining room

If this is a room used solely for eating it wastes valuable space since eating occupies much less time than this room could be used for. Ideally it would also be used as a children's play area in the western sector and the toys could be put away in cupboards when guests come to dine. A study or work

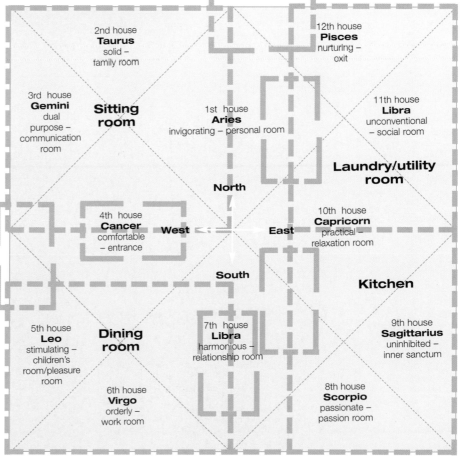

area could be created in the southern sector and more practical use of the space thus achieved. The harmonious area of relationships falls partly in this area and partly in the kitchen and passageway between. This is good if chores and duties are shared, which is likely in this well-balanced arrangement.

Kitchen

This room probably presents more problems than the others put together, unless the occupant likes cooking and sex a great deal. Their possible pooja room – the 9th house, the Sagittarius area of the uninhibited inner sanctum – is located here in the kitchen. This could work if they combine cooking and meditation, which is indeed possible and is regarded as one of the sacred arts in India.

But their passionate area – 8th house, Scorpio – is also located here. I leave it to you to use your imagination to work out how these two key features could be combined here. Part of the kitchen is also taken up with their 10th house – the Capricorn relaxation room. This would work if the kitchen table is located here and friends could gather round it for coffee and a chat. Alternatively, one could have a nice comfortable chair, perhaps in front of the wood-burning stove, and a shelf of favourite books.

Laundry room/utility room

This room incorporates the social room – not usually possible in a laundry room – and the exit of the 12th house, Pisces. It could be that the exit of dirt from clothes is important to this person or it may be that they need to utilize this space better. It would be recommended that this room is partitioned to make better use of its potential.

Making changes

You would need to go through the same process for the upper floors and for each individual room. Let's take an example of how we might look at an individual room. From this diagram there are various points one could make about the arrangement of furniture within the room.

- The north-west corner should be where the seating is placed, to incorporate the family area and the communication area (TV and telephone). The door, ideally, would be located along the middle of the west wall to accord with the comfortable entrance of the 4th house.

- A personal space should be created in the north to enhance the personal room aspect.

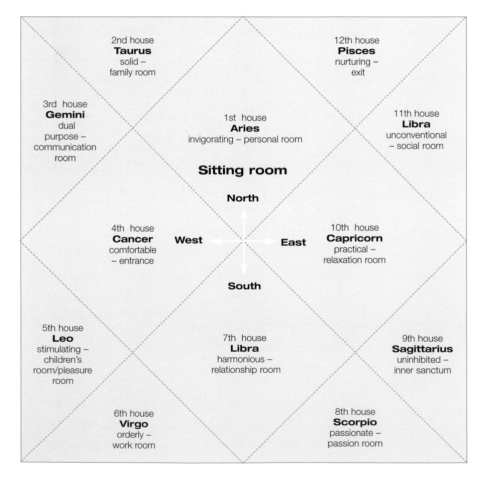

2nd house **Taurus** solid – family room		12th house **Pisces** nurturing – exit
3rd house **Gemini** dual purpose – communication room	1st house **Aries** invigorating – personal room **Sitting room** North West ← → East South	11th house **Libra** unconventional – social room
	4th house **Cancer** comfortable – entrance	10th house **Capricorn** practical – relaxation room
5th house **Leo** stimulating – children's room/pleasure room	7th house **Libra** harmonious – relationship room	9th house **Sagittarius** uninhibited – inner sanctum
6th house **Virgo** orderly – work room	8th house **Scorpio** passionate – passion room	

- The children's toys and equipment should be located in the south-west corner, with a work space alongside so that an adult can keep an eye on the children while working.
- The east wall should be private and here one could create a shrine if there was no space in the house for a pooja room.
- There could perhaps be a dining area in the north-east for friends to gather round – this would satisfy the social area of the 11th house.
- For the relaxation aspect of the 10th house perhaps a reclining armchair could be provided.
- In the relationship area there could be a photo of the two partners, while the passionate area would be located along the right-hand side of the south wall – perhaps with a reclining sofa?

Doing it for yourself

There is an old saying:

Give a man a fish and you feed him for a day.

Teach him to fish and you feed him for a lifetime.

I am not going to give you a fish, but rather teach you to fish. These room alignments can be worked out for any ascendant sign – but, as I said earlier, you have to do some of the work yourself. You will learn and remember more if you do it yourself, so I am not going to work through all the twelve ascendants. In Chapter 7, the practical section, we will work through some more examples as we put the whole package together. For now this is enough *jyotish* for you to be going on with. But if you want to take it up as a subject you will find a lifetime's rewarding study.

vaastu
for buildings

We need to look briefly at the original formal rules of Vaastu before we move on to its practical application. Traditional Vaastu can be quite unnerving because it doesn't see shades of grey – merely black and white. If something is wrong, according to the vedic instructions for Vaastu, then it is wrong.

For instance, the rules might say that an extension built in the south-west area of your home means financial loss and defamation. But I bet there are a lot of people living in homes with south-west extensions who have never been subjected to either.

Understanding the tradition

Traditional Vaastu can be a little too extreme. It also doesn't really make any recommendations as to how to change or improve things if you are unfortunate enough to have bought a house with an extension in the south-west – except perhaps to demolish the whole thing and start again. But even this is bad Vaastu because the *Vedas* say you can't build on a site where a house has stood before or you inherit all the bad luck of the previous occupants or owners.

So you can't rebuild and you can't make changes: what are you going to do? Don't worry for the moment. We will look later at adapting traditional Vaastu to a more modern way of living – and updating it. Remember that Vaastu was conceived as an architectural science, to be put into place before you built your house. And if you were building your house in India it became the family home. Here in the West we move a lot more than people did in ancient India, where the same family would have occupied the same house for generations – and still do in a lot of cases. Traditional Vaastu says get it right and there is no need to move. There may well be something in that. Here in the West we seem to suffer from a sort of restless spirit syndrome, whereby we constantly move in order to satisfy some restless urge to make things better. Perhaps if we got it right at the beginning we could relax a bit more and enjoy living right where we are. Perhaps our spirit is restless because it is not being given sufficient attention, not having the right flow of energy to make it alive and vital.

Vaastu seems to have such essential elements to it that I feel it has something important to say to us in this age of instant gratification. Both where we live and how we live are important. If we constantly seek change to make things better, we might be well advised to look at the cause rather than seeking a different place to be wrong in each time.

In the next chapter we can lighten it all up a bit and make some of the prognosis a little less threatening, scary and dogmatic. But first we need to understand something of the general rules, so perhaps you'd like to ignore the overdramatic prognosis.

Selection of site

The first aspect of any building – the ground – should receive more consideration than the other aspects. Before building, we need to examine the basic site to make sure drainage, light, location and space are optimum. Therefore, the following basic guidelines should be carefully observed.

Directional alignment

The geometrical axis of the plot should be properly aligned with the axis of the earth's magnetic field – i.e. one set of boundaries of a plot should be parallel to the north/south axis and the other set of boundary lines should be parallel to east/west axis. We looked at this in an earlier chapter.

In this diagram alignments AB are north/south and alignments CD are east/west.

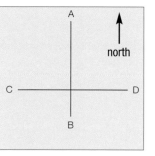

Correct alignment

If the property is not parallel to the magnetic axis, such land is said to be poor for overall growth, peace and happiness. Hence any plots having directional non-alignment, as shown below, should be avoided.

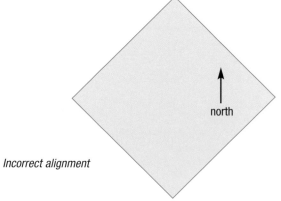

Incorrect alignment

Slope of land surface

The land should be elevated towards the south and west sides and lower in the north and east sides, for overall growth and happiness. A slope in any other direction can cause various disadvantages:

- If the land is high in the north or east directions, it causes financial losses or can damage the potential of the owner's sons or other male children.
- If the land is low in the south-east direction, it causes financial loss, ill-health, short life, sorrow and loss due to fire.
  - If low in the southern direction, it causes illness and short life.
  - If low in the south-west direction, it causes loss due to theft and unwanted expenses, illness and short life.
  - If low towards the west, it causes sorrow and unhappiness, financial loss, defamation and is not good for children's health or growth.
  - If low in the north-west direction, it causes financial loss and mental unrest.
  - If low in the centre, it causes various troubles.

The last one of these seems fairly obvious – it means your house is sinking!

Size and shape of site

A square site is ideal. If the ratio of two adjacent sides of a site is 1:1 and every corner is a 90° angle, it is called a square and this is best for overall growth. If the ratio of width and depth of a site is within 1:15 and all corners are a 90° angle, this rectangular shape is also good for growth. If the depth is more than twice the width, however, the site becomes weaker for growth.

Regular shapes: Having a regular, symmetrical shape is considered better than an irregular shape. The unsymmetrical shape is not always good. There are obviously endless permutations of regular shapes, but here are some of the most common ones:

- Square shape – overall growth
- Rectangular shape – overall growth
- Circular shape – increases mental capabilities
- Hexagonal shape – prosperity

Irregular shapes:

- Any oval shape – inauspicious (That's all it says in the vedic literature. Inauspicious simply means that it won't kill you but it won't do you any good either.)
- Any triangular shape – loss due to fire, government harassment, penalty.
- Any parallelogram shape – financial losses, quarrels in family.
- Any star-shaped plots or buildings – quarrel and litigation, destruction of peace.
- Any trident-shaped plots or buildings – quarrel, loss of peace.
- Any shapes using both straight lines and curves – tragic death or imprisonment.
- Any bow-shaped buildings – various troubles, fear of enemies.

Location of extensions

Building on an extension to an existing building is, according to Vaastu principles, never a good idea, but some locations are better than others. So, if you have to, then choose carefully.

- Extension in north – good for growth and all-round prosperity.
- Extension in east – good for fame and success
- Extension in south – causes loss of wealth.
- Extension in west – causes loss of health.
- Extension in north-east – good all round for health and wealth.
- Extension in south-east – good for success but money slow to come in.
- Extension in south-west – bad all round for health and wealth.
- Extension in north-west – good for money but bad for health.

Missing parts of a building

If your basic square shape, which is most preferable, has chunks missing out of it, then it is considered inauspicious indeed. It is known as a deformation of shape or form and is considered not a good idea at all.

This irregular-shaped but colourful building is in Buenos Aires.

Piece missing from north-east corner of square plot or building

- Piece missing in north-east – poor for financial growth, health and peace.
- Piece missing in north-west – unhappiness, enmity and loss of wealth.
- Piece missing in south-east – financial loss, loss of reputation and unhappiness.
- Piece missing in south-west – mental unrest, ill health, financial loss and loss of position or reputation.

Principles of roads next to building or plot

We looked briefly in Chapter 3 about having a road next to or running alongside your plot of land or building. Here are the Vaastu principles of roads:

Two roads and roads adjoining a plot

- Single side road or road on north side of the plot – good.
- Road on east side of the plot – good.
- Road on south side of the plot – good.
- Road on west side of the plot – neither good nor bad.
- Double roads adjoining the plot – neither good nor bad.
- Roads on both north and east sides of the plot – very good.

- Roads on both east and south sides of the plot – poor.
- Roads on both south and west sides of the plot – neither good nor bad.
- Roads on both west and north sides of the plot – neither good nor bad.
- Roads on both north and south sides of the plot – neither good nor bad.
- Roads on both east and west sides of the plot – neither good nor bad.

Roads adjoining three sides of a plot

- Roads on three sides of the plot except east side – poor.
- Roads on three sides of the plot except south side – poor.
- Roads on three sides of the plot except west side – poor.
- Roads on three sides of the plot except north side – poor.

Roads adjoining all four sides of the plot

- Roads on all the four sides of the plot – very good.
- Plot at the junction of four roads on all sides – not good.
- Junction roads on any three sides of the plot – not good.
- Junction roads on any two sides of the plot. – not good.
- Junction or 'T' road on any one side of the plot – not good.
- Plot at the dead end of the road – very bad.

Trees

In India the Vaastu of trees is considered important. Obviously the vedic literature contains the names of a great many trees. I'm afraid that I can't find out what these are in English. It could be that they aren't known outside of their native India or that they are simply not translatable into English. In India they may have another, more common name, which might make it easier to identify them, but our climate might not be suitable for growing such trees anyway. The names are given here for information and interest. The basic principles of where and how to plant trees remains the same, even if we use different species.

The following trees are amongst the principal ones mentioned and should be planted in particular locations:

- Peepal – good on west side of the house, bad on east side of the house.
- Bargad – good on east side of the house, bad on west side of the house.
- Goolar – good on north side of the house, bad on south side of the house.

The shadow of any tree should not fall upon the house between 9 am and 3 pm. What this means is that trees should be located well away from the house. This makes sense because trees can undermine buildings with their roots and cause damage if their branches fall in storms. We will look at this in more detail later in Chapter 8.

Wells, hillocks and temples

Here are a few other principles, concerning wells, hillocks and temples. Obviously a lot of these will simply not apply to Western homes – but then again they just might.

- There should not be any well or public tank (I don't think we have a lot of these any more) near the site in south, south-west, north-west, south-east, west or east areas.

- The shadow of the house should not fall on the well between 9 am and 3 pm.
- There should not be any river or wide canal on the south or west sides of the site.
- If a river or canal is on the east side of the site and the flow of water is from south to north, it is good.
- Similarly, if the river or canal is on the north side of the site and water flows from west to east, it is also good.
- If there are hills or hillocks on the south, south-west and west sides of the site, it is good; otherwise, it is weak for growth.
- The shadow of any temple or other place of worship should not fall upon the site from 9 am to 3 pm.
- Further, the temples of Sun, Brahma, Vishnu and Shiva should not be in front of the site. Durga temples should not be on the left or right sides of the site. Jain temples should not be at the back of the site.
- There should not be any graveyard, burial ground or tomb adjacent to or at the back or in front of the site.
- The compound walls should either be of the same height or have the south wall higher than the north wall and the west wall higher than the east wall.
- If the plot has two or more roads adjacent to it, the gate should be provided in the smaller side.

Gates

The location of gates is very important in Vaastu. Obviously we can't all have magnificent estates with huge wrought-iron gates. But invariably we do have some kind of gate, even if it's a little humble wooden affair. Here is a chart showing the different locations and what they mean. Again, this is traditional Vaastu and should be taken with a very large pinch of salt.

What you should do is divide your plot or garden into 64 squares – the traditional mandala form – and this gives you some 30 positions for gates. Some positions are good, some are bad. Move the gate if it falls in a bad location.

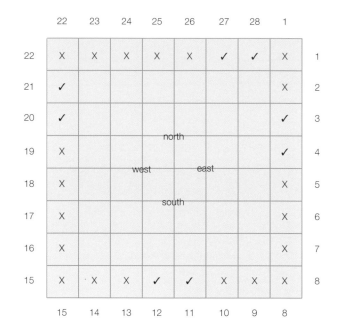

	22	23	24	25	26	27	28	1	
22	X	X	X	X	X	✓	✓	X	1
21	✓							X	2
20	✓							✓	3
19	X			north				✓	4
18	X			west	east			X	5
17	X			south				X	6
16	X							X	7
15	X	· X	X	✓	✓	X	X	X	8
	15	14	13	12	11	10	9	8	

East side

1. Loss due to fire
2. Female growth
3. Prosperity
4. Government favour
5. Disruption to working life
6. False indictment
7. Cruelty or unpleasantness
8. Loss due to burglary

South side

8. Loss due to burglary
9. Loss due to fire
10. Rebelliousness
11. Generosity
12. Prosperity, human growth
13. Unfavourable
14. Lack of appreciation
15. Financial loss

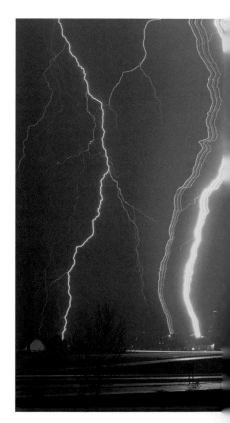

West side

15. Financial loss

16. Damage to potential of children

17. Trouble to children, unwanted expenses

18. Antagonism

19. Financial loss

20. Financial and human growth

21. Financial and human growth

22. Government persecution

North side

22. Government persecution

23. Financial loss

24. Disease

25. Tragic death, accidental injury, imprisonment

26. Hate

27. Happiness

28. Financial gain, human growth

Obstacles

And if you have an obstacle in front of the gate this too will lead to all manner of illness, loss and unhappiness – apart from causing you to bump into things, that is. An obstacle in front of your gate is known in India as *dvar-vedh* and obviously you should move any obstacles that impede access to the gate.

- If you have a road impeding access to your gate then your longevity is threatened (I told you the original Vaastu was scary).
- A tree blocking the gate – damage to children.
- Corner of another house or building – mental disease.
- A well – mental disease.
- A pillar or column – defects in females.
- A gutter or mud-pit or puddles – sorrow.
- Water drainage – unwanted expense.
- A temple – destruction of growth.
- Staircase or railings – unhappiness.

However, if the distance between the door and the obstacle is great enough, or if a public road is between the door and the cause of obstruction, the effect of the obstacle is nullified.

Wells, boreholes and underground tanks

The good zones for siting a well, a borehole or an underground water tank in the plot are as follows:

- North-east – overall increase and strength.
- East – financial gains.
- West – financial gains.
- North – happiness.

Similarly, the unfavourable locations are:

- South-east – injury to children.
- South – injury to wife.
- South-west – harm to owner.
- North-west – antagonism, mental disorder, financial loss.
- Centre – lack of wealth (your house is sinking again).

Building design

Location of building in the plot

As we saw in Chapter 3, the main body of the house should lie either symmetrically in the centre of the plot or nearer to south and west sides, leaving more open space on north and east sides.

Size of the building

In general, the ratio of sides – width to depth – should be either 1:1 or 1:1.5 or 1:2.

Shape

There should not be any pieces missing or extensions, except for balconies and porches, in the basic square or rectangular shape of the building.

Floor levels

The floor level in the south-west, south, west, south-east and north-west zones should not be sunken or low down. Similarly, the levels in the east, north-east and north zones should not be higher or raised. The level in the central zone should be neither low nor raised. There can be split levels in the central zone.

Highest and lowest parts of the building

Either the building should have the same height in all parts or the south-west, south and west parts of the building should be highest, keeping terraces on north and east sides. The north-east or north or east sides should never be higher than south and west sides. Also, there should be symmetry in projections and elevations.

Roof slope

If the roof slopes, the slopes should be symmetrical. If the slope is on a single side, it should be down towards north or east.

Doors

Size and shape

Doors, which are known in Hindi as *brahmsthan*, form a very important part of Vaastu because they allow the easy access of energy or block its exit. Normally, the width of a door should be half its height. Here are a few rules about doors and door openings:

- The door should not be too high, too low, too wide or too narrow.
- Square doors should be avoided.
- The door frame should be rectangular and any arch should be set above the door frame.

- The total number of doors on a floor should be in even numbers and ones which don't end in zero (not 10, 20 or 30, but rather 12, 24 or 34).
- Similarly, the number of windows should also be in even numbers not ending in zero.
- The upper line of all doors and windows should be in the same horizontal level, except for that of the main door of the building, which can be higher than the other doors.

Obstructions

Obstructions are known as *dvar-vedh*, as we saw earlier. There should not be any obstruction in front of any door caused by wall corners, staircase railing, pillar or columns, or partial overlapping of another door frame. There should also not be any overhead obstruction of the door frame by any perpendicular beam or edge.

Mutual alignment of two consecutive doors

There are four types of door alignment and these are shown below.

Utsang (straight): If the outer door opens in the same direction as that of an inner door, it is called *utsang* and is supposed to be the best alignment.

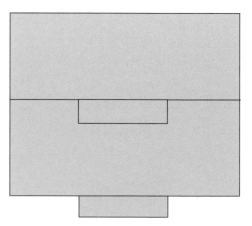

Utsang

Savya (right-hand side): If the outer door is situated to the right hand of the inner door, it is called *savya* and is good.

Prishtha-bhanga (showing the back): If the inner door is located opposite the reverse side of the outer door, it is called *prishtha-bhanga* and is inauspicious – bad luck indeed.

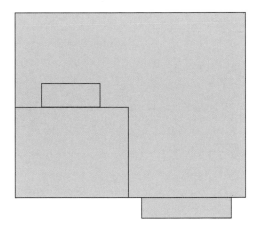

Savya

Prishtha-bhanga

Ap-savya (left-hand side): If the outer door is situated to the left hand of the inner door, it is called *ap-savya* and is also good.

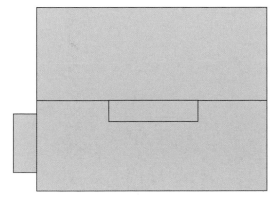

Ap-savya

Staircase

The staircase should be provided in the west or north sides of a building. The turnings should be in a clockwise (right-hand) direction while climbing up. On emerging at the upper floor, the facing should be towards the south or east. The number of risers should be such odd numbers, so that if divided by 3, the balance is always 2.

Inner planning of a house

Fireplaces

Fireplaces have their own special place in Vaastu and there are good and bad locations. Providing a fireplace in the south-east corner of a house – or room – is regarded as the best location. Fireplaces should not be situated under or above the pooja room, or a lavatory, or where the bed is placed.

The location of the pooja room

If the pooja room cannot be centrally located or if an entire room cannot be dedicated to it, then a pooja shrine should be built in the north-east corner of the house or room. There are various Indian gods that have their rightful place and direction:

- Brahma, Vishnu, Shiva and Jinendra can face towards any of the four directions.
- Indira, Surya and Kartikeya should face towards east or west directions.
- Ganesh, Kuber, Bhairava, Chamunda and Hanuman should face towards the south-west direction.

Lavatories

I'm not sure that flushing WCs were around when the *Vedas* were being written, but ancient India had its own method of disposing of night waste. I have adapted the traditional Vaastu locations to incorporate modern lavatories. The guidance is as follows:

- The lavatory should not be provided above or under the pooja room or shrine, a fireplace or where the bed goes.
- The facing of the lavatory (when you are sitting down on it) should be either towards the north or towards the west.

Bedrooms

Bedrooms should be located in auspicious places, as follows:

- The main bedroom should be in the south-west direction or nearest to south-west.
- Children's bedrooms should be towards the north or east of the main bedroom.
- Guest bedrooms should be in the north-west area of the house.
- The head of the bed should be located in the south or east direction.

There should not be any beam, storage cabinet, or split surface of ceiling above the bed location. The bed should not be placed in extreme corners of the room.

Interior planning of an office or study

If you work from home, and more of us do these days, then a study should be provided in the south-west area or nearest to the south-west area. In the perfect Vaastu configuration your study would be set out as follows:

- You would have the door in the north-east corner, facing north
- You would sit in the south-west corner, facing north
- Any visitors would be seated facing south.
- A comfortable sofa would be located facing west.

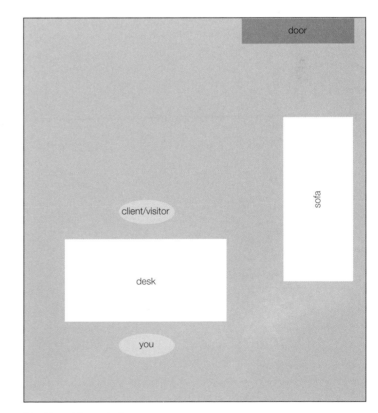

Ideal layout for a study

Bringing the past into the present

There is a lot of information in the *Vedas* concerning Vaastu, most of which I feel is irrelevant to modern house construction, design and living. In the next chapter we will put the elements together and fuse them into modern Vaastu, which is real and practical. The traditional Vaastu may well be fascinating but time has moved on somewhat. The sort of thing I am skipping is text like this:

> *Dashnina is the South and Yama is its Lord. Its elephant is Vamanam. Its demon is Gundothara. These three guard this direction and if the dweller is properly constituted he will escape from the envy of others and cast off all evil eyes.*

It's intriguing, but not a lot of use if all you want to do is sort out your flat or decorate your semi. So we won't deal with the lords, elephants or demons in the next section. But we will deal with fabrics, furnishings, colour schemes, style and the proper flow of energy, to enable you to take from Vaastu the essential ingredients, without having to become a Hindu or wear a sari.

practical
vaastu

There has been a lot of information for you to absorb, understand and digest. If you have persevered thus far, then well done – and I shall look forward to guiding you through the next section on how to put it all together and do it for yourself. If you have turned to this section first in the hope of skipping all the theory, then go back, go back. There is simply no point in implementing changes if you don't know why you are doing it.

You must have a basic grounding in the principles or it will all be gobbledegook and unintelligible. Chances are some of it will be anyway, even if you've read every word and understood all of it.

I have been researching Vaastu for about four years now and I still lose my way at times, since it is a very inexact science based on a system laid down a very long time ago. For instance, we all have to incorporate elements of electricity into our homes to power our televisions and computers, lights and cookers and heaters.

Stabling for the elephants

But what did Vaastu say about such a vital energy force all that time ago? Why, nothing of course. But it did go into the location of your servants' halls, granaries and armouries in great detail. Now, I don't have any servants, nor do I have a granary and I have no sword, shield, bow and arrow or lance to hang up. Nor do I need stabling for my elephants or store rooms for the palanquins. I don't

need cages for the peacocks or watch towers to protect me from marauding bands of brigands and bandits. What I need is to free up some energy, create a harmonious environment and make my life smooth and easy. I want to improve my finances, luck, relationships, health and general well-being. I bet it's pretty much the same for you.

Working with what we've got

So that's what we are going to do. That's what we are going to concentrate on. We'll skip the elephants and the granaries, ignore the armouries and the peacock houses. Let's work only with what we've got – a Western lifestyle and a Western housing system.

We are about to embark on a journey to a better way of living. Along the way we shall incorporate elements of Vaastu, as well as being practical and full of common sense about it. If, for instance, Vaastu principles say that the street light you've got outside your front gate means your third cousin once removed is going to have a bad day, then we'll live with that. But if the street light being where it is means you bang your head or crack your shins on it every morning as you rush out to work, then we'll deal with it by moving the gate, phoning the council to complain or learning to leave more time so we don't rush so much in the mornings. That's common sense. Worrying about your cousin's bad day isn't.

Vaastu comes from a very old culture steeped in exotic traditions that we simply have no experience of. To us in the West, a car, computer, phone, TV, dishwasher and MDF shelving have more relevance than a Maharishi's palace, saris, the caste system, worshipping Ganesh, cooking with ghee and bathing in the Ganges. So let's embark on a journey of discovery into modern Vaastu, where we incorporate the essential elements but don't become superstitious or fanatical.

First things first

Let's do a quick recap. We have explored the principles of Vaastu and taken account of the 'good' and 'bad' compass alignments. We have learnt a little about *jyotish* and can calculate our ascendant, so we know the astrological layout of our home. And we have explored *ayurveda*, so we understand the way energy moves through our home and we know our own and our home's *dosha*.

Now we can begin to put these together. But first we have to understand our home thoroughly. We have to move through it as if we were the vital energy of life itself. And we need to begin outside – outside the boundaries of our home entirely.

Outside the boundaries

Go outside now and make a note of the following:

- What do you see as you face your home?
- In what direction does your front gate/entrance face? (This means the direction you are facing if you turn your back on the gate or entrance and face away from the house.)
- What roads do you have nearby?
- If you were energy attempting to enter your home, would your progress be impeded or helped? Would the flow of energy be easy or difficult? For instance, do you have to climb over

several bicycles left in the hallway of a flat? Does the gate open easily or does it require a lot of pushing because it is stiff and needs oiling?

- If you turn your back on the entrance or gate what can you see? What sort of view do you have? What sort of energy is flowing towards you?

Energy picks up the resonance of whatever it has passed through or over on its way to you. If it has recently passed through an abattoir or charnel house, prison or cemetery, then it will have picked up emotional echoes that it will bring to you. If it has passed over a beautiful stretch of countryside or a meandering river, or even recently passed along clean and well-kept streets, then it will bring with it that energy too.

You might not be able to do much about this view, this resonance of energy, but we are on a journey of exploration and discovery and it is useful to know and understand that where you live is having an effect on your emotional senses. If you want to cause change to occur in your life you have to be very aware of the detail of your existence – and this means knowing what you are living near. If you feel positively unhelped by such an energy presentation, then you may well have to move to a better location.

The direction of your home

In Vaastu, the direction your home faces is determined by the direction your front door faces. In an ideal world this will be the same direction as your gate or entrance. The direction is all-important as it categorizes what sort of home you are living in. This is based on the ascendant signs we looked at earlier. There are judged to be twelve directions – four important ones (south, east, west and north) and eight of lesser importance (north-west, west-north, west-south, south-west, south-east, east-south, east-north, north-east). These eight lesser directions may not be as you would expect to see on a Western compass, but in Vaastu that is the way they are described. A diagram may explain this more easily.

You will notice that this diagram is very similar to the horoscope charts of the ascendant we were looking at earlier. It's the same basic layout. You may also notice that unless your front door is spot on and exactly in the middle of the west, east, north or south wall, it gets allocated to another direction which occupies a greater space. So although the eight directions of lesser importance occupy more space, they are not so auspicious as the four major ones which occupy very little space indeed along the boundaries. For the purposes of the next exercise, I would advise allowing

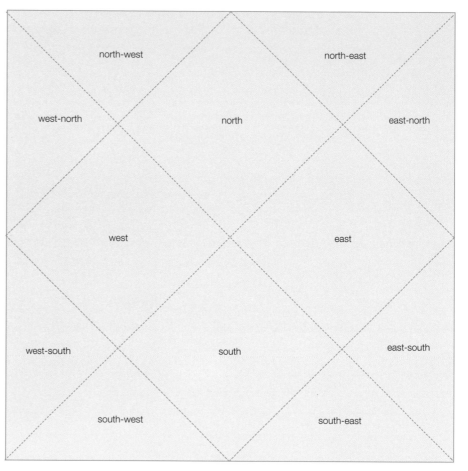

The positions of the 12 directions

yourself a little leeway; so, if your front door falls within the middle third of the wall, you can allow it as one of the four important directions. For internal room arrangements you need to stick to the original layout, but for doors we can move the boundaries a little.

Having worked out in which direction your door faces, you need to know what this means. Each of these twelve directions is linked to one of the twelve ascendant signs we looked at earlier. Each of these

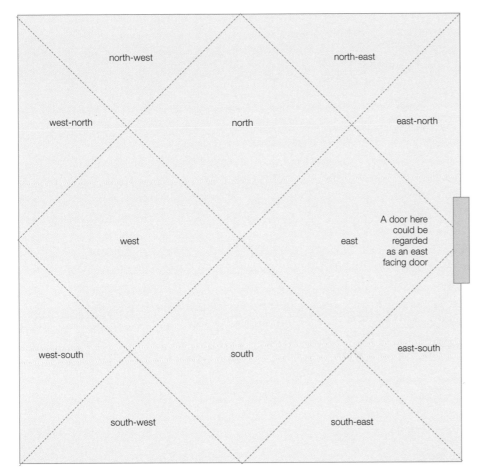

north-west

north-east

west-north

north

east-north

west

east

A door here could be regarded as an east facing door

west-south

south

east-south

south-west

south-east

signs has a key word to summon up its essential element and is linked to a specific direction:

Aries – invigorating/north

Taurus – solid/north-west

Gemini – dual-purpose/west-north

Cancer – comfortable/west

Leo – stimulating/west-south

Virgo – orderly/south-west

Libra – harmonious/south

Scorpio – passionate/south-east

Sagittarius – uninhibited/east-south

Capricorn – practical/east

Aquarius – unconventional/east-north

Pisces – nurturing/north-east

This will give you an idea of how your home would be classified according to Vaastu principles. Let's suppose you live in an east-north house. This direction relates to Aquarius. Aquarius is known for its unconventionality, its originality, its independence, its unpredictable nature. Does that match up to how you see your house?

Work out your house direction and match it to its zodiac sign. Each of these zodiac signs means something and you will help your house by treating it accordingly. Thus the Aquarius house will respond better if it is given its head and allowed to be wacky and unconventional. It will feel uneasy being straight-jacketed into a conventional existence.

Matching your ascendant to the house's ascendant

Now you need to match your ascendant to your house. This will give you two key words to work with. Suppose you are a Cancer ascendant and live in a north-west house, the Taurus house. Cancer is comfortable and Taurus is solid. These two key words should be at the back of your mind when it comes to decorating, furnishing and living in the house. By doing this you are taking both yourself and your house into consideration and merging the two – fusing the elements of both of you. And that's fusing the elements, not confusing the elephants!

The *dosha* of the house

Referring back to the earlier chapters, you now need to work out the *dosha* of the house – and your own, of course. In the same way that you matched the house ascendant and your own ascendant, you can now match the two *dosha* to see whether you are compatible.

Once you have done this you need to use the front door direction, along with the ascendant zodiac sign, to find out what sort of energy is flowing into your house. It will be one of four elements; space energy occupies the central part of the house and is regarded as the energy as it leaves rather than as it arrives.

To remind you, the five elements with their compass directions are:

- North to west – air
- North to east – water
- East to south – fire
- South to west – earth
- Central – space

As we saw earlier, the elements have different characteristics. Here is a reminder:

Aakasha – *space*

This element incorporates all the cosmic energies, such as gravitational forces, magnetic fields and heat and light waves. Its main characteristic is known as *shabd*, which could be translated as 'sound'.

Vaayu – *air*

This element is the atmosphere around us, what we breath and what transmits *prana* – universal breath. Its main characteristic is *sparsh* – touch.

Agni – *fire*

This element represents the heat and light of fires, lightning, volcanoes, as well as the heat of fevers, energy, passion and vigour. Its main characteristic is *roop* – form.

Jala – *water*

This element represents everything liquid – rain, rivers, the sea, as well as steam and clouds. It also represents all living plant material and its main characteristic is *ras* – taste.

Bhumi – *earth*

This element represents all solid matter, as well as everything we stand on – the earth itself. It is also the element of quality – *gun*.

Key words

So now you can work out what energy is entering your home, how it is affected by the zodiac sign and what it does to you. For this you need to know the key words for each of these features: your

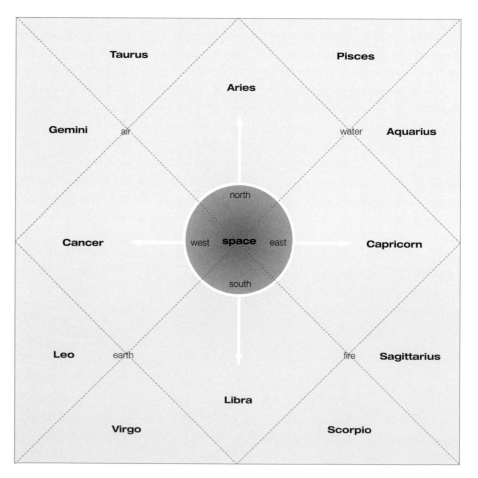

ascendant sign, the ascendant sign of your house (according to the direction it faces) and the type of energy entering your home. The key words for the four possible elemental energies entering your home are:

- *Vaayu* – air – **movement**
- *Agni* – fire – **vitality**
- *Jala* – water – **nourishing**
- *Bhumni* – earth – **solidity**

You must remember that the attributes of these elements extends far beyond these key words. These are there to help you, to crystallize your thinking about the elements, but they do not represent them in their entirety.

Elaine and her house

Let's work through an example. Elaine has Scorpio as her ascendant – key word *passion*. Her house faces due west, the sign of Cancer – key word *comfort*. The energy entering her home through her front door is a combination of air – *movement* – and earth – *solidity*. Thus she has four key words to work with – *passion*, *comfort*, *movement*, *solidity*. Her house is a modern detached house standing in its own grounds. She earns her living as a graphic designer. She works from home and is divorced with one child.

Her key words

What can we learn from her four key words that will help her in decor and furnishings? Well, she needs passion in her colour schemes, so lots of red and rich colours. She needs comfort, so lots of luxurious fabrics and high-quality furnishings. Her energies are movement and solidity. She needs to be grounded but also free to work around schedules and not be tied to a regular routine. She needs to work for herself of course, and she needs some form of stability, which having a child will provide –

she has to be there to pick them up from school, and that sort of thing.

Creating her environment

Elaine loves her house, which is turn-of-the-century (the last one, of course) and she has furnished it in a mock Victorian style, with lots of rich velvet curtains and cushions, leather sofas and desk lamps throwing passionate pools of light across deep red surfaces.

Elaine's dosha

Her *dosha* is *vata* – creative, changeable, energetic, quick, restless, sometimes anxious and fearful, liking warmth and sleeping badly. The *dosha* of her house is also *vata*, which seems quite compatible indeed. She feels comfortable (her front door direction) in her home, but wants to improve her chances of having another relationship, though a more successful one. The recommendation is to work on her relationship area – the Libra or south area. Here she has been using an old store room to keep her files and artist's equipment. She has now cleared this out and painted the room blue to encourage harmony and she is using the space as a small pooja room. She feels that her next relationship should be with her karmic soulmate, so she is combining the pooja room with her relationship area to augment this desire.

Seeing how it works

The above example will give you an idea of how all the features of Vaastu fit together. Obviously you will need to do this for yourself and your own home. You need to know:

- your ascendant;
- the house's zodiac direction from the front door;
- the *dosha* of the house;
- your *dosha*;
- the key words for all the above.

Once you have this information you can work out what your house represents about you. Then you can do the same exercise for each room in the house until you have understood the Vaastu of the entire building. Each room needs to be understood from both its direction (the way the door faces) and its location according to the zodiac sign it occupies.

With the example of Elaine, we can use her chart to gain quite a lot of information, as the diagram here shows.

Adding in some earth

If Elaine wants to attract her soulmate she needs to add an element of Taurus into her Libra area of relationships. Key word for Taurus? That's right – solidity. Her pooja room needs to have some solid foundation to make this work for her. She needs to introduce the element of earth here – some rocks, stones, pebbles – to make it solid. At the moment she has too many candles (meaning too much fire), too much water and too much clear, white space (meaning too much *prana*). By adding in the solid element of rocks she will transform this area and make it compatible both with the two zodiac signs of Libra and Taurus, but also with the earth/fire *ayurveda* elements. Large pieces of basalt, which have been through the fires of the earth, would be ideal rather than beach-washed pebbles, which would only seem more watery.

Looking at the detail

Once we have completed this exercise we can move on to do it for each room. First we need to see the chart – in this case Elaine's – overlaid on to a ground plan of the house. In this way room structure will become apparent and we will be able to see where conflicts might arise and where harmony should be expected.

Once we've got the overall chart we can look closely at any problem areas first. Now we know that Elaine wants to improve

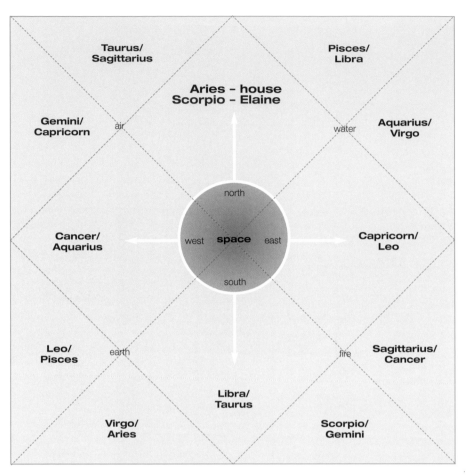

Elaine's chart

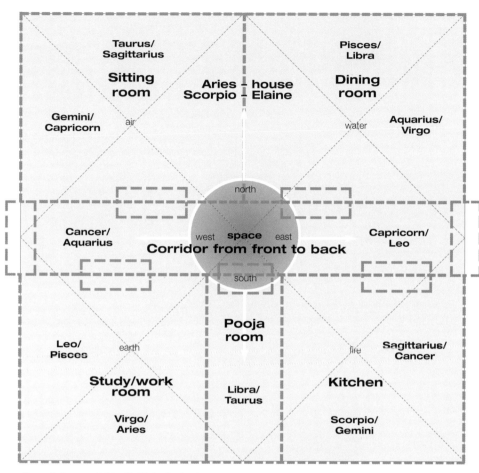

Taurus/Sagittarius		**Pisces/Libra**
Sitting room	**Aries – house Scorpio – Elaine**	**Dining room**
Gemini/Capricorn	air	water	**Aquarius/Virgo**

north

Cancer/Aquarius	west space east	**Capricorn/Leo**
	Corridor from front to back	

south

Leo/Pisces	earth	fire	**Sagittarius/Cancer**
Study/work room	**Pooja room**	**Kitchen**
Virgo/Aries	**Libra/Taurus**	**Scorpio/Gemini**

Ground plan overlaid with Elaine's chart

her chances of a successful relationship and we have made recommendations as to how to improve her pooja room. But what else can be improved? What else can we spot that might need checking or looking into?

Making best use of the elements

For a start, Elaine's sitting room – which occupies the air position – and her study/work area – which occupies the earth position – could perhaps be swapped round. Energy starts its movement through the house via earth, fire, water and air, and lastly moves through the central area of space.

This left-hand spiral of energy is worth remembering because it affects all aspects of Vaastu. The key points are:

- Energy flows in a spiral.
- Energy flows anticlockwise.
- Energy gets lighter nearer the centre.
- Energy gets faster nearer the centre.
- Energy undergoes a transformation as it spirals from earth to space via fire, water and air.

So if Elaine located her study area in the element of air, it would give her more energy, faster energy, lighter energy and be more conducive to work. Having her sitting room in her earth element area would enable her to relax more as that energy is heavier, slower and more languid.

Elaine's new study

But before we all rush off and change rooms, we need to check the *jyotish* of such a change. Her study would occupy, in its new place, the house's *jyotish* of Taurus and Gemini – key words *solidity* and *dual purpose*. Her own *jyotish* would be Sagittarius and Capricorn – *freedom* and *practicality*. Combine

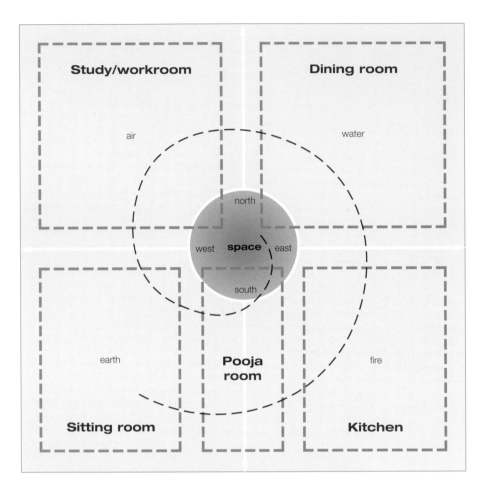

this with the element of air – fast, clear energy – and you have a good room to work in, especially if you work from home (freedom), need to meet deadlines (solidity), are involved in creative but practical work (practicality) and need the study to double up as a designer's study, accounts office, reading room and child's homework place (dual-purpose).

Elaine's new sitting room

Her sitting room, on the other hand, becomes more earthy and the house's *jyotish* of Leo and Virgo – stimulating and orderly – go hand in hand with her own *jyotish* for this area of Pisces and Aries – nurturing and invigorating. This is the room both to relax and be nurtured in, and also to converse and discuss, be challenged by friends and have sparkling conversations with prospective soulmates. But it is also a room to keep neat and orderly (which suits Elaine's fairly tidy nature) and to spend pleasant evenings in.

Change and compatibility

Are you getting the hang of this now? Check the elements against the house's *jyotish* and your own. Look up the key words for each area and room. Make sure it is all compatible. Don't make any changes until you have seen the ramifications across each and every aspect of Vaastu.

Unlike *feng shui*, there is no simple cure like hanging up a mirror or installing a wind chime. In Vaastu it is much more complex, much more interwoven. Nothing can change until you take the step towards that change by wanting to transform not only the environment but also yourself.

And that's just for the inside of the house: in the final chapter we'll look at Vaastu for gardens.

garden Vaastu

In Vaastu, all the same principles apply whether you are designing a house, a garden, a multiplex cinema, a shopping mall or a humble garden shed.

Now with traditional Vaastu we have the *Vedas* to guide us through the intricate labyrinth of principles and essentials – and we have historic evidence in the form of ancient buildings now being excavated at such archaeological sites in the Indus Valley as Mohenjodaro and Harappa. But with gardens it is not so easy. They don't last so long. They leave little behind in the way of archaeology or evidence. They are, by their very nature, impermanent and transitory.

What we can glean about garden Vaastu comes from the Mogul conquerors of India, with whom the Aryans shared a common ancestry – that of the ancient Persians. By piecing together the intricate strands of Islamic garden design and the principles of Vaastu as applied to buildings, we can learn quite a lot about ancient Indian gardens.

Most of the buildings surviving from pre-Islamic times are temples because, until a fairly late period, temples were generally the only buildings constructed of stone. The remains of some palaces also exist, particularly their stone foundations.

The *purusha* mandala

The basis for the construction of a temple is the mandala – the Vaastu *purusha* mandala. Given the geometric and symmetric

layout of mandalas, you would expect the layout of a temple and its gardens to be equally geometric, and this is what we find.

The mandala and the temple are representations of the world or the cosmos, with humankind superimposed on it in the form of a human figure (see page 51). The basic plan of the temple is the square or rectangle, though often all we are left with is a linear axis outline. Where a temple is found within an enclosed space, this is in most cases a rectangular space aligned with the temple. In many instances a water feature is found, often as a tank within the temple compound. The alignment of the temple with the compass directions emphasizes its basis in the world. There is always water present in some form, for washing and for symbolic purposes.

Among the best examples of these elements in the Indian subcontinent are the Surya temple at Modhera, the Minaksi temple at Madurai, and the Harimandir at Amritsar. The symbolism is probably at its most elaborate at Angkor Wat, in Cambodia.

garden surrounding it. For religious reasons, as we saw earlier, these representations are more common in Hindu temples than in Buddhist ones.

Other important buildings, including palaces, would have had designed landscapes and gardens associated with them. However, there are few early palaces left, or even any traces of them. One that does remain is the outline of the formal gardens of a palace, from about 450 CE, at Sigiriya in Sri Lanka. This has a strong square layout, based on the axis of the palace. The remains of other palaces can be seen in their foundations, such as in the stone bases to the palace pillars in the royal centre of Vijayanagara. There are references to town, house and palace gardens in the *Vedas* but no detailed drawings, unfortunately.

There are many references to forests, forest glades, and flower-filled clearings in the passages about life in the forests in the *Puranas* and the epics of Hindu literature. Typically these mention

Landscape elements

Temple complexes may contain representations of other landscape elements, although it is not clear that these were always present in pre-Islamic times. Representations of forests occur as well as representations of rivers – either in the temple itself, in the shape of a god or goddesses, or as carvings of rivers on the temple or in the

RIGHT: Water features don't have to be as grand or as imposing as this but, ideally, they should be based on the square.
LEFT: Angkor Wat ruins, still the spiritual home of Cambodia's Buddhist monks.

flowering creepers, shady trees, singing birds, fragrant flowers, and ponds, often associated with an *ashram* or other simple dwelling. They are common in the accounts of the exiles of the principal characters of the *Ramayana* and the *Mahabharata*, and in the accounts of the lives of the sages.

These descriptions occur in such number and detail that it is apparent that an informal garden based on a forest clearing, and probably by a river or stream, was seen as an ideal. Of course any such garden or dwelling would have been submerged in the forest almost as soon as the gardener gave up, so these accounts will probably have to remain the chief evidence. Subsidiary evidence can be seen in the detail of some paintings. In some cases, accounts of informal gardens are given in relation to cities, or in the immediate neighbourhood of cities.

The two traditions of gardens

It appears from this, that there were two different traditions of garden and landscape design in pre-Islamic India, which could be called the formal and the informal traditions. The formal is based on the geometric surrounds of a civic building, aligned with the compass directions, and is focused on the mandala and cosmic order. The informal is based on the forest clearing and relates to the simple life of a forest dweller living as part of nature.

Islamic gardens

Most of the gardens of the various Islamic cultures are traditionally lumped together under the title 'Islamic gardens'. The common square pattern of the garden or the compound of a tomb probably developed from a fusion of the walled garden, thought to have

Working in the garden can be a chore or a spiritual meditation – one is hard work, one is easy.

originated in the Persian *paradiaza*, and the Garden of Eden, described in the Book of Genesis in the Bible, a legendary place from which four rivers flowed out in the four cardinal directions. A *paradiaza* is a walled enclosure that shuts out the outside world and encloses a garden. The fusion of these two styles developed into the *chahar bagh*, which is Persian for quartered garden. The first known walled tomb garden in India is Sikander Lodi's tomb in Delhi, predating the Mogul tomb gardens.

The Indian *chahar bagh*

In the main, the *chahar bagh* as seen in India is a square or rectangular enclosure, quartered by water channels that are said to represent the four rivers of energy flowing into the central place

occupied by space – universal energy. Examples of these include the principal Mogul tombs – Sikandra, Taj Mahal and Humayun's tomb. These show a layout that could be called the Indian layout of the *chahar bagh*: the garden is enclosed within walls, is square or nearly so, and has a central reference point, usually the tomb. Water is present outside mosques for the same reason as outside temples: the worshipper is required to be clean before worship.

Formal gardens

Other formal garden layouts exist. A common one is the linear garden (such as Shalamar bagh, Kashmir, and some of the gardens in the Alhambra, Spain). These may blend into the squared layout, as in the *chahar bagh* of Esfahan. The garden may

It can therefore be seen that there are distinct parallels and similarities in several key areas between ancient Indian concepts and Western concepts. The main points of these similarities are:

- a square or rectangular enclosure, often a walled compound;

- the presence of a dominant focal feature, such as a temple tower, tomb, pond or palace;

- a quartering or other division of the near landscape, often along the cardinal directions;

- the use of water as both an ornamental and an essential washing feature.

Creating your garden

This should give you enough information to enable you to plan your Vaastu garden. Try to create the central square shape, divided into the four quarters. Align your garden – where possible – along the north–south/east–west axis. Create a central feature of water

be part of the surrounding landscape or town. The garden could be divided into numerous squares, as in the Aram bagh (Rambagh), Agra.

In Europe, one line of garden tradition is derived directly from the Islamic interpretations of the Garden of Eden. Later on there were attempts to find ideas in Roman and Greek thoughts, and later still in Chinese and Japanese traditions.

to symbolize the element of space and to create a focal point for your garden. Keep hedges and bushes low so that the entire garden can be seen at once.

If you have a long, thin garden you can break it up into a series of squares. Likewise, if you have an irregular shape, break it down into smaller units, each being a square shape or as near as you can get to it.

A gazebo as a focal point

You might like to add a very authentic Indian design feature – the gazebo. The word actually comes from the Persian and means a platform or raised area for viewing the Moon. Originally gazebos were constructed in the corners of the garden for people to sit out at night and watch the Moon and stars. These gazebos would have been partly covered and they would have had a hole in the centre from which the occupants could look upwards and see the night sky. The position of gazebos changed to become a central focal point, often reached by crossing a small bridge over one of the four rivers. You might like to recreate this feature, but bear in mind that a Western climate might not be quite so suitable for sitting out at night and watching the Moon. But it's worth a try anyway, and more useful in summer than in winter perhaps. I have one and it doubles as a summerhouse, storage space for the croquet set, and children's toy store.

Planting

In a traditional Vaastu garden, shade would have been essential, so plane trees, cypresses and fruit trees were planted. These fruit trees are the same as those mentioned in the Qur'an as a description of paradise. Flowers were grown in sunken beds so that they didn't impede the overall view of the garden. They were often also planted around the base of the trees, which were placed on the outside edges of the garden – again, so as not to impede the view of the whole garden. The traditional plants chosen were opium poppies, roses, narcissus, mallow, anemones, violets and lilies – all plants which will also do well in a milder climate such as ours. Grape vines were grown to cover trees and buildings. You may have some success with these; if not, use climbing jasmine instead.

Some basic guidelines

If you want to create the perfect Vaastu garden, you might like to follow these guidelines:

- Use a square shape as far as possible; divide up irregular or rectangular plots into smaller units of squares.
- Divide the square into four quarters.
- Use flagstone paths along a north–south/east–west axis to represent the four rivers.
- Have sunken flowerbeds planted with some of the plants mentioned here and let them all self-seed.
- Create a central pool or fountain – traditionally painted blue.
- Install a gazebo for watching the Moon.
- Plant orange trees in terracotta pots and clip them into ball shapes.
- Plant trees along the outside edges of the garden for privacy. Use cherry, plum, almond, apple and peach trees – with these you will get blossom, scent and fruit.
- Turf the four quarters in grass.

I hope you enjoy your Vaastu garden and that you have understood enough of the principles of Vaastu to recharge your home and invigorate your life. It is truly a vast subject and the search for perfect peace and tranquillity in our lives should begin now.

If you are not for yourself, what are you for?

index

acknowledgements

The publishers would like to thank the following sources for their kind permission to reproduce the pictures in this book:

AKG: 5t, 23, 30r (Jean Louis Nou) 33 (British Library) 70/71, 79, 89l & r (Bibliotheque Nationale), 90 (Bibliotheque Nationale)

Carlton Books: Graham Atkins-Hughes 9 main, 9 t, 133/ Polly Wreford 0, 115, 118/119, 130 / Mel Yates/Tom Leighton 116

Caroline Jones: 5, 6/7, 10/11, 21, 24/5, 29, 31, 32, 34, 64 t, 65, 64 b, 72/73, 81, 91 b, 100/1,122, 137

Corbis: 51, 44, 77 c, 77 r, /Richard Hamilton Smith 108 / Roger Ressmeyer 77, 78 l / Nik Wheeler 0 b / Patrick Ward 42, 43

Getty One Stone: 16, 29 b, 86, 92, 132, 136 / Ben Edwards 74 /Nicholas DeVore 2, 4ct, 26/27, / John Elk 4 t, 14/15, / Paul Harris 4 b , 52/53 /James Strachan 18, 28, 35/ Robert Van der Hilst 30

Image Bank: 0 t /Steve Allen 20 /John Banagan 103 / A Boccaccio 24 t / Mike Brinson 57 t, /Van Butselle 85 / Alain Choisnet 19 r / Color Day 110/111 / Alan Danaher 91 t / Stuart Dee 19 l / Joe Devenney 13 / Steve Dunwell 105, 106 / Anthony Edwards 44, 54 /In Focus International 58 b, 60 r / Don Klump 17 / / David de Lossy 5 b, 88 t , 134/135 /Rita Maas 57 b, / Nino Mascardi 61 b / Eric Meola 47 b / Steve Murez 56 , 138 / Joseph Van Os 128/129 r / Nicki Pardo 88 b /Andrea Pistolesi 104, 112 / Terje Rakke 59 /D. Redfearn 141 / Steve Satushek 81 / Pete Turner 48 / Franklin Wagner 49 / Stephen Wilkes 22, 22 main/ Yellow Dog Productions 66 /67, 82

Ray Main/ Mainstream: 1, 3, 9 b, 39, 46 b, 47 t, 48, 40, 50 (Designer Nana Ditzel), 58, 62, 68, 69, 76, 97, 99 (Mathmos), 114 (Ozwald Boateng), 139, 140

Narratives: Jan Baldwin 4 cb, 12, 36/37 main, 38, 44 br, 44 tl, 44 cl, 46 tr, 60 l, 63, 81 b, 96, 107, 109, 119 r, 113, 123, 124, 127, 128, 131 / Peter Dixon 44 bl, 44 bc / Nicola Hill 8 / Tamsyn Hill 61 t / Polly Wreford 5cb, 120/121